Anonymous

Final examination questions given by the state boards to the junior and senior classes of the state normal schools of Pennsylvania

Anonymous

Final examination questions given by the state boards to the junior and senior classes of the state normal schools of Pennsylvania

ISBN/EAN: 9783337274689

Printed in Europe, USA, Canada, Australia, Japan

Cover: Foto ©Paul-Georg Meister /pixelio.de

More available books at **www.hansebooks.com**

EXAMINATION QUESTIONS

Given by the State Examining Boards to the Junior and Senior Classes of the State Normal Schools of Pennsylvania.

For STUDENTS and TEACHERS.

Compiled by
THE SCHOOL GAZETTE,
Ex-Superintendent L. S. Shimmell, Editor.

HARRISBURG, PA.:
THE GAZETTE PUBLISHING COMPANY,
1894.

This Book is Dedicated to the

Alumni of the

Pennsylvania State Normal Schools.

(4)

INTRODUCTORY.

THE general purpose of these questions is the common purpose of all questions; namely, to awaken curiosity, stimulate inquiry and promote investigation. Teachers and pupils both are moved to greater mental activity by a book that interrogates them on their studies from many different standpoints. A more specific purpose which these questions have is to delineate the course of study as laid down by the State of Pennsylvania for the professional preparation of the teachers. It is hoped that they may serve to show those teachers who are but poorly equipped for their work, the way to a professional education. Finally, like all others of its kind, this book will be of daily service to the teacher in furnishing questions for reviews and examinations, and it will assist the applicant for examination in preparing himself thoroughly for that ordeal.

Acknowledgment of favors is due the Normal School Principals who so kindly granted the use of the questions given at their respective schools.

GAZETTE PUBLISHING COMPANY.

HARRISBURG, PA., 1894.

(6)

TABLE OF CONTENTS.

Junior Questions.

	PAGE.
1. ENGLISH GRAMMAR AND COMPOSITION,	10
2. RHETORIC,	22
3. LATIN,	33
4. ORTHOGRAPHY,	41
5. READING,	53
6. SCHOOL MANAGEMENT,	59
7. GEOGRAPHY,	65
8. HISTORY OF THE UNITED STATES,	81
9. CIVIL GOVERNMENT,	95
10. PHYSIOLOGY AND HYGIENE,	105
11. VOCAL MUSIC,	114
12. BOOK-KEEPING,	120
13. DRAWING,	126
14. ARITHMETIC,	131
15. ALGEBRA,	147

Senior Questions.

16. ENGLISH LITERATURE,	163
17. LATIN,	169
18. PSYCHOLOGY,	181
19. METHODS OF INSTRUCTION,	193
20. HISTORY OF EDUCATION,	203
21. NATURAL PHILOSOPHY,	209
22. BOTANY,	221
23. GEOMETRY,	233
ANNOUNCEMENT,	248

(8)

I. ENGLISH GRAMMAR AND COMPOSITION.

The Structure of the Language, Letter-Writing, Punctuation and Such Composition as Will be of Use in Daily Life, Form the Work in Grammar and Composition.

English Grammar and Composition.

EXAMINATION I.

1. What is meant by the *properties* of a word? Part of speech? Name the parts of speech and the properties belonging to each.

2. Distinguish between personal and relative pronouns. Name the relatives and state a rule for the use of each.

3. Select all the pronouns in the following sentences, naming the sub-class, and government of each: (1) What can I do for you? (2) Which boy did this? (3) I know who you are. (4) You can take whichever one you please. (5) As many as came were accommodated.

4. Write five sentences illustrating five uses of *that*.

5. Correct the errors in the following, giving reasons: (1) I think it to be she who helped me. (2) Neither Charles nor his brother ate their breakfast this morning. (3) Which is the more preferable. (4) I neglected to have mentioned the fact. (5) I never saw a more perfect specimen. (6) If I was wealthy I should build a hospital for the poor. (7) He reads first-rate but he spells poor. (8) I hope you shall not feel badly if you do not pass.

6. Name and illustrate three uses each of participles and infinitives.

7. Distinguish between active and passive voice and state the voice of the following verbs: (1) The pupil should be encouraged. (2) The boys were running home. (3) They laughed at him. (4) Let me die the death of the righteous. (5) Do pay attention.

8. Diagram: *This* was the noblest Roman of them *all*:
All the conspirators, *save* only *he*,
Did *that* they did in envy of great Caesar;
He only, in a general-honest thought
And common good to all, *made one* of them.
His life was gentle, and the element
So *mix'd* in him *that* Nature might *stand* up
And *say* to all the world—"This was a man."

9. Parse briefly the words in italics.

10. Write a letter applying for a position as teacher in Ebensburg. Address R. R. Davis, Sec.

EXAMINATION II.

1. Define: Etymology, Syntax, Language, Grammar.

2. Name the different functions of the pronoun and give examples of each.

3. Paraphrase the following:
Under a spreading chestnut tree
The village smithy stands;
The smith, a mighty man is he,
With large and sinewy hands;
And the muscles of his brawny arms
Are strong as iron bands.

4. A man should never be ashamed *to own* that he has been in the *wrong*, which *is but saying* in other words that he is wiser to-day than he *was* yesterday.

    1. Classify the clauses in the above sentence as principal and subordinate.

    2. How is the predicate of the principal clause modified?

    3. Name the predicates of the subordinate clauses and tell by what each is modified.

    4. Parse words in italics.

    5. Diagram the sentence.

5. Write a sentence whose predicate is modified by an adverb, a phrase, and a clause.

6 (a) Write a sentence using the word "flowed," and another, using the word "flown."

(b) Write synopsis (first person, singular number) of the verb *be* in the indicative mode.

EXAMINATION III.

1. Define English Grammar. A verb. A conjunctive adverb. A participle. Mood. Inflection. Syntax.

2. Write the possessive singular and plural of *brother-in-law, chief, deer, empress, goose, hero, lady, ox, tyro, wife.* Write the principal parts of *am, begin, lay, sing, work.*

3. Analyze the following sentences:
   1. *For us* to know our faults is *profitable.*
   2. He bears him *like* a portly *gentleman;*
      And, to say truth, Verona brags of him
      To be a virtuous and well-governed *youth.*
   3. Beneath those rugged elms, that yew-tree's shade,
      Where heaves the turf in many a mouldering heap,
      Each in his narrow cell forever *laid,*
      The rude forefathers of the hamlets sleep.

4. Parse the italicized words in the foregoing sentences.

5. Write a letter to the Principal, stating the relation that grammar bears to other language studies.

EXAMINATION IV.

1. (a) Analyze the following sentence:—A man should never be ashamed to *own that* he has been in the wrong, *which* is but *saying* in other words that he is wiser to-day *than he* was yesterday.

   (b) Parse italicized words.

2. Define "inflection" as used in grammar. To what extent is English an inflected language?

3. Name three substantive uses of a subordinate clause, and give an example of each.

4. Write the possessive plural of wolf, child, hero, father-in-law, President Adams, he, and who.

5. Define relative pronoun, conjugation, comparison of adjectives, and analysis.

6. (a) Write a synopsis of the verb *teach* in the third person, plural number, indicative and potential moods.

(b) Give active, passive, and progressive participles of the same verb.

7. Give principal parts of lay, lie [to recline], fly, flow, over-flow, undo, and bid.

8. Define voice. How are verbs in the passive voice formed? How in the progressive form?

9. Correct errors and give reasons:

(a) No person was ever so unkind to me.

(b) She is one of those women that always has some fault to find.

(c) Sufficient data was not given to solve the problem.

10. Write a letter to a board of School Directors, making application for a school.

EXAMINATION V.

1. Explain briefly but fully how personal and relative pronouns differ.

2. Explain the active and the passive voice, and use the verb *sink* in both.

3. How to form the plural number of all kinds of nouns, letters, signs, etc.

4. How to form the possessive case, singular and plural in all cases.

5. Write the plural possessive of thief, princess, prince, sheep, son-in-law, vertebra, he, I, who, herself.

6. Principal parts of lie (two meanings) sit, lay, set, swim, flee.

7. Correct the errors, if any appear, in these sentences, giving a pointed but brief view:

(a) Must I that has been faithful now lay down and die.
(b) But what saith the Scriptures, and who art thou that claim such authority.
(c) He become glad when he seen the army were draw up in line.
(d) One or the other of you have a new pair of gloves.

8. Best method of acquiring a full vocabulary.
9. Make an outline for a composition on *How to study*.
10. Write a dozen lines about some book recently read.
11. Who decides what is correct and incorrect in the use of oral and written language?

EXAMINATION VI.

Under a spreading chestnut tree
　The village *smithy stands;*
The *smith*, a mighty man is he,
　With large and sinewy hands;
And the muscles of his brawny arms
　Are strong as iron bands.

1. Classify this sentence.
2. Diagram the first two lines.
3. Point out figure of syntax, if any.
4. Parse italicized words.

Correct if wrong: (1) I will sell the horse to you reasonable. (2) His father was opposed to him entering the army. (3) I supposed it to be him. (4) I supposed that it was he. (5) He thinks he knows it, but he don't. (6) It doesn't pay to make mistakes.

EXAMINATION VII.

1. Define a phrase, a clause, a simple sentence, a compound sentence and a complex sentence.
2. Decline the following: father-in-law, jugful, beef, hero, mouse.
3. Give the principal parts of the following verbs: do, see, lie, lay, set, sit.

4. Give a synopsis of the verb *to see*, first person plural, of all moods, active voice, all tenses.

5. How is the passive voice formed? conjugate the verb "to teach," in the present subjunctive passive.

6. Form the plural of the following nouns · parenthesis, criterion, ally, alley, half, motto, alkali, life, cupful.

7. Parse the *italicized* words in the following sentences: The *sun rising* we walked five *miles* farther.
What conscience dictates to be done, *do* without question.

8. Diagram: (a) Whoever succeeds will earn what they offer. (b) His being an Englishman gave him his freedom an hour later (c) To become a famous orator like Demosthenes, the Athenian, is a task requiring genius and years of toil.

9. Correct and give reasons.
(a) I have not saw him to-day.
(b) He done the work himself.
(c) He gave it to we girls.
(d) It wasn't her.
(e) There was two boys and three girls.

EXAMINATION VIII.

1. Define a sentence, a clause, a phrase, a word, a letter, a punctuation mark, parsing, analysis, "Language Lessons" and grammar.

2. Write the following correctly, with special regard to capital letters, punctuation marks and the reason for them, and the equivalents of abbreviations:

a page of gibbons decline and fall of the roman empire was read by superintendent baer to hon J P Wickersham ll d when they were in paris

3. Give the plural of *lady, valley, mouthful, antithesis, genus.* Compare *last, badly, wisely, polite, next.* Give the *principal parts* of *drink, flow, fly, sit, set.*

4. Write a compound sentence; change it to a complex; and again so as to contain a participial phrase.

5. Analyze the following, and parse the italicized words:
"*Cyriack*, this three years' *day* these eyes, though clear,
To outward view, of blemish or of spot,
Bereft of light, their seeing *have forgot;*
Nor to their idle orbs doth *sight* appear
Of sun, or moon, or star, throughout the year,
Or man, or *woman*."

EXAMINATION IX.

"The chariest maid is *prodigal enough*,
If she *unmask* her beauty to the moon;
Virtue *itself* scapes not calumnious strokes.
The canker galls the infants of the spring,
Too oft before their buttons *be disclos'd;*
And in the morn and liquid dew of youth
Contagious blastments are most imminent."

1. Analyze the sixth and seventh lines. (2) Parse the words *underscored*. (3) Decline "their" and "maid;" compare "chariest." (4) Write a synopsis of "disclos'd" in the first person, indicative active, progressive form, and passive. (5) How is it determined whether "strokes" is a noun or a verb, "before" a preposition or an adverb?

EXAMINATION X.

Parse italicized words.
Would it be worth the having or the *giving*—
The *boon* of endless breath?
Ah, for the weariness *that comes* of living
There is no cure *but* death.
Ours were indeed a *fate deserving pity*,
Were that sweet rest *denied;*
And few, *methinks*, would care to find the city
Where never any died.

EXAMINATION XI.

1. Illustrate and define a sentence.
2. Write a complex sentence; a compound sentence.
3. "Between broad fields of wheat and corn, is the lowly home where I was born."
Analyze the above sentence.
4. Parse the words "corn," "is," "where," "I."
5. Define case and number of pronouns.
6. Define person and number of verbs.
7. Form the plural of *turkey, armful, footman, sheep*.
8. Form the possessive case of *tyro, fox, baby, flowers*
9. Write the synopsis of the verb *do*, using the subject *he*.
10. Supply the correct form of the personal pronoun, first person, singular number, in the two following sentences: This is between you and —. He knew it was —. Please let John and — go.
11. What verbs have the passive voice, and how is it formed?
12. Write a short letter to the Superintendent of Schools of this county, asking for a position.

EXAMINATION XII.

1. Define the terms: verbal, pleonasm, ellipsis and attribute, and illustrate each by giving an example.
2. Discuss the elements of a sentence with reference to their rank, their structure, and their function.
3. Write examples of complex sentences containing the noun clause used respectively as subject, object, complement of the subject and appositive.
4. Specify the advantages in using the *passive voice* and illustrate with example.
5. Supply subject and verb to the following expressions, and note the loss and gain by the addition:
Why so unkind?

6. Correct and give reasons—Let him be whom he may. This is not such a warm day as yesterday.

7. Write short paragraphs upon the following subjects: Examinations, Free Trade, General Sheridan.

EXAMINATION XIII.

1. What parts of speech are capable of inflection?
2. What is the inflection of the various parts called?
3. What is the fundamental difference between adjective and adverbial modifiers?
4. Write a classification of the pronoun.
5. Make sentences, using the following words in the possessive plural forms: foot, thou, woman and lady.
6. What is the use of modifiers in a sentence?
7. Write a sentence in which each essential element is modified. Underscore each modifier and tell its function.
8. Write a synopsis of the verb *write* in the passive voice.
9. Arrange in natural order and parse the italicized words—

"*Yet* a few days, and thee
The all-beholding sun shall see no more
In all his course; nor *yet* in the cold ground
Where thy pale form was laid with many tears,
Nor in the *embrace* of ocean shall exist
Thy *image*."

10. Analyze and parse italicized words:

"The wise man applauds *him whom* he thinks most virtuous; the rest of the world, him who is most wealthy."

EXAMINATION XIV.

1. What is the underlying principle on which the classification of the parts of speech is based?
2. Write a sentence containing a substantive clause in which there is a compound relative pronoun in the objective case.

3. The office of what part of speech does the clause you have just written, perform in the sentence?

4. Write a sentence containing a noun used absolutely in the nominative (nominative absolute) and performing the office of an adverb.

5. Analyze the following sentence and parse the words in italics: "*Lives there who* loves his *pain.*

EXAMINATION XV.

1. Define Grammar. A sentence. A phrase. An infinitive. Inflection. Case. Subjunctive mood.

2. Write the following words in the possessive case, in both numbers: *brother, commander in-chief, daisy, foot-passenger, negro, she, valley.* Write the principal parts of *burn, fly, lie* (recline), *lose, row.* Write the following adjectives in the different degrees of comparison: *ill, fragrant, late, old, under.*

3. Analyze the following sentences:

(a) Bless'd are those
 Whose blood and judgment are *so* well commingled
 That they are not a pipe for fortune's finger
 To sound what stop she please.

(b) *Washington's refusing* to be President the third *time* proved him *to be* a true statesman.

(c) Triumph Arch, that fill'st the sky
 When clouds prepare to part,
 I *ask* not proud Philosohpy
 To teach *me what* thou art.

4. Parse the italicized words in the foregoing sentences.

5. Write a letter to the examiner, giving him some idea of when and how you would begin to teach grammar.

2. RHETORIC.

This Branch Includes Manner of Expression and Criticism of Original Work, Together with the Principles of the Subject Which Prepare the Student for the Work in Literature, Which is Taken up in the Senior Year.

RHETORIC.

EXAMINATION I.

1. Define rhetoric, diction, figure of speech.
2. What are the rhetorical qualities of a good sentence. Define each.
3. Define periodical, loose, and balanced sentence.
4. Define metaphor, synecdoche, irony, metonymy, personification, and give an example of each.
5. Name the figures in the following: (a) Am I a Roman slave? (b) Death is swallowed up in victory. Oh death, where is thy sting? (c) It is not an uncommon fact. (d) The white light of truth. (e) He aspired to be the highest above the people, above the authorities, above the laws, above the country.

EXAMINATION II.

1. What is diction? What are the essential qualities of a good diction?
2. What rules should guide us in the choice of words? Illustrate.
3. Name the figures of speech. Define and illustrate three of them.
4. What is an epic poem? An allegory? A comedy? A sonnet? Blank verse?

EXAMINATION III.

1. Arrange in verse and punctuate,—
   "Hast thou no friend to set thy mind abroach good sense will stagnate thoughts shut up want air and spoil like bales unopened to the sun."

2. Point out and define the figures of speech in the above lines.

3. Write ten or more lines upon the thought suggested by the quotation.

4. What are the essential requisites of good style?

5. Distinguish between wit and humor; purity and propriety of diction; rhyme and rhythm.

EXAMINATION IV.

1. Discuss "Use is the law of language."

2. What rules should guide a writer in the choice of words?

3. What are the essentials of a good narrative ?

4. What is meant by style? What is the style of Longfellow? Macaulay? Wordsworth?

5. Write a brief sketch of *The Merchant of Venice. Comus.*

NOTE.—This list was headed "Rhetoric and Literature."— *Publishers.*

EXAMINATION V.

1. Name and illustrate four figures of speech.

2. Give three rules for the use of capitals, and illustrate.

3. What's the difference between long meter and short meter?

4. What should be the qualities of a good style? Explain and illustrate the terms employed.

5. Tell, in brief, the story of "The Merchant of Venice." Which character do you most admire, and why?

6. Discuss—

"Gayly the old man sang to the vibrant sound of his fiddle;
And anon with his wooden shoes beat time to the music.
Merrily, merrily whirled the wheels of the dizzying dances,

Under the orchard trees and down the path to the meadows,
Old folks and young together, and children mingled among them."

EXAMINATION VI.

1. For what purpose do you study rhetoric? How is it related to grammar? To logic?
2. Name the essentials of good diction. Define barbarism, solecism, style, redundancy and verbosity.
3. What should be applied to a word to determine its purity? Discriminate between the words—healthy and healthful; bring and fetch; trustworthy and reliable.
4. What are the rhetorical qualities of a good sentence? Define each.
5. Why is figurative language used? Define *four* rhetorical figures and illustrate each.
6. Give rhetorical classification of sentences, with several rules for their construction.
7. Define different kinds of poetry. Name the different kinds of poetic feet. Illustrate each kind by a word.
8. Tell what you can about correct letter writing.
9. Write an application to John Jones, Esq., secretary of the school board, Harrisburg, Pa., for a position as teacher. State all the facts that the school board should know in considering application.

EXAMINATION VII.

1. How does rhetoric differ from grammar and logic?
2. Name in order the parts of an oration.
3. Define style and name its essential elements.
4. Name the figures of speech in the following. (a) Ye are the light of the world. (b) And there are many other things which Jesus did, the which, if they should be written every one, I suppose that even the world itself could not contain the books that should be written.

5. Define taste and give directions for its improvement.
6. In what respect does poetry differ from prose, and what is its mission?

EXAMINATION VIII.

1. Define: Rhetoric, style, diction, paucity, redundancy and provincialisms.
2. What tests should be applied to a word to determine its purity? Discriminate between the words: bring, carry, take and fetch.
3. Define figure of speech, name and give example of several kinds of figures.
4. State law of verbal formation—Name an accepted word formed contrary to this law.
5. Give rhetorical classification of sentences, with several rules for construction of sentence.

EXAMINATION IX.

1. Define rhetoric and give the derivation of the word.
2. (a) What is a figure of speech?
   (b) Name the most common ones and an example of each.
3. Scan the following, name the kind of feet, and verse used:

There's a dance of leaves in that aspen bower,
There's a titter of winds in that beechen tree,
There's a smile on the fruit, and a smile on the flower,
And a laugh from the brook that runs to the sea.

4. Define poetry, and name the different kinds of poetical composition.
5. Give the different classes of prose composition and name an example of each.
6. (a) What is the importance of unity?
   (b) Give rules for securing it.

EXAMINATION X.

1. Wherein does rhetoric differ from grammar?
2. What do you include under the term *invention?*
3. What are the essential qualities of *style?*
4. Write half a page upon "Franklin," using the figures *hyperbole, metaphor, simile* and *metonymy.*
5. How can *energy* be secured?
6. Name four kinds of poetry, and show how it differs from prose.

EXAMINATION XI.

"The chariest maid is *prodigal enough,*
 If she *unmask* her beauty to the moon;
Virtue *itself* scapes not calumnious stroke,
 The canker galls the infants of the spring,
 Too oft before their buttons *be disclos'd;*
  And in the morn and liquid dew of youth
 Contagious blastments are most imminent.

1. Scan the first three lines, naming foot and metre and marking their quantity.
2. This being an extract from Hamlet, designate and define the kind of poetry it is, and name the author.
3. Name and define the figures of rhetoric in the fourth and fifth lines.
4. Which would be likely to use more figurative language, a Sioux chief or Geo. Bancroft? Give a reason for your answer.
5. Define the essential properties of style.
6. How does a barbarism differ from a solecism?
7. Discriminate *maid* and *girl; enough* and *sufficient; infant, babe* and *child.*
8. Define rhetoric and defend the study of it.

EXAMINATION XII.

1 Definition and derivation of the term *rhetoric.*
2. What is meant by perspicuity in words?

3. Give definition of the following: Parallel, diallage. What is meant by irony, sarcasm, innuendo?

4. Difference between the three departments of harmony.

5. What is method? What various forms does subject-matter assume?

6. Name the four chief classes into which the various kinds of composition are divided? Cite examples of each.

7. What is meant by emotions? Classify them.

8. Difference between the ancient and modern idea of the beautiful.

9. What is meant by the ridiculous? What are the three requisites of wit? What is the squib? The pasquinade? The bonmot? The lampoon?

10. What is literature in its most general signification. What are the seven departments of literature? Define poetry. What metres are employed in the following? Mark off the feet:

> *God help* you, sailors, at your need —
> Spare the curse;
> For some ships safe in port, *indeed*,
> Rot and rust,
> Run to dust."

EXAMINATION XIII.

1. What is rhetoric, and what is its relation to grammar? to composition?

2 Assume that you are about to write an exhaustive paper upon the subject of 'Energy of Style,' and then write an outline suitable to be the framework of your paper.

3. Write a loose sentence and also a period; then compare these two forms of the sentence so as to show the difference of structure.

4. Write each of the following without any figure after-

ward name the figure used in each as given, and lastly, show why the figurative form is the better:
1. "She sat like patience on a monument smiling at grief."
2. "Sleep, gentle Sleep, nature's soft nurse, how have I frightened thee that thou no more wilt weigh my eyelids down!"
3. "For fools rush in where angels fear to tread."
5. Discuss wit and humor.
6. Outline the subject, prose productions.
7. Explain how you would proceed in the preparation of a paper upon any given subject.
8. Discuss poetry.

EXAMINATION XIV.

1. What is meant by style? What is the style of Macaulay? Burns? Dickens? Washington Irving? A good daily newspaper?
2. Discuss the origin of figurative language. How should figures be used?
3. Discuss the standard of taste.
4. Discuss wit and humor. Name some witty productions, and their authors. Some humorous productions, and their authors.
5. Write a brief sketch of Shakespeare's *Julius Caesar*.

EXAMINATION XV.

1. Give one rule each for the use of the comma; semicolon; period; exclamation point.
2. What is purity and to what is it opposed?
3. Give one of the ways in which clearness may be violated; emphasis; unity; strength; harmony.
4. Define and illustrate simile; metaphor. Give one rule each for their use.
5. Discuss rhetorically. And the Dr. told the sexton and the sexton tolled the bell.

EXAMINATION XVI.

1. Discuss "Usage is the law of language."
2. Explain in full how we come naturally to use figures of rhetoric. Illustrate.
3. Discuss wit and humor. Distinguish them. Mention some wits and humorists among literary men.
4. Explain what is meant by style. Characterize the style of Washington, Irving, Goldsmith, Macaulay, Milton.
5. Discuss force or energy.

EXAMINATION XVII.

1. Define rhetoric, invention, style, prose, poetry, a figure.
2 Name and define three kinds of prose, and name one author noted for each. Same of poetry and authors.
3. Name some English Epic and discuss it.
4. Define and compare metaphor, simile and allegory. Give example of each.
5. Give the origin of the English language. Name and discuss three English authors before Shakespeare.

EXAMINATION XVIII.

1. Define figures of rhetoric and name the principal figures.
2. Define simile and state its laws.
3. Define metaphor and state its laws.
4. Define beauty and give its elements.
5. Define sublimity.
6. In poetry define foot, verse, stanza, rhyme and blank verse.
7. Name and define the different kinds of verse and give an example of each.
8. Name and define the different kinds of poetry.
9. Select one or two stanzas of poetry and discuss the same rhetorically.

EXAMINATION XIV.

1. (a) Define rhetoric.
   (b) In what sense is it an art? Two extreme views have been held in regard to the province of rhetoric: first that it is limited in its use to invention, or the art of finding something to say; secondly, that it is limited to the mere decoration and ornament of discourse.
   (c) Show wherein these definitions are defective.
2. (a) Under what division of Rhetoric is punctuation included?
   (b) Give reasons for the use of the dash.
   (c) What is the relative importance of the marks of parenthesis? the dash? and the comma?
   (d) The omission of the comma after "plums," in the following sentence, would have what effect on the meaning of the sentence? "There are apples, pears, and plums, which never ripen."
3. Make the necessary corrections in the following sentences, and state clearly your reason for each correction :
   (a) Fashion for the most part is the ostentation of Riches
   (b) Now a man now a seraph now a beast
   (c) There are five moods the indicative the potential the subjunctive imperative and the infinitive
   (d) Bacon Francis usually known as Lord Bacon was born in London England Jan 22 1560 and died 1626 he was famous as a scholar a wit a lawyer a judge a statesman and politician.
4. Define the following terms: Diction, barbarism, law of verbal formation, property, precision, pedantry, affectation.
5. (a) What is a periodic sentence?
   (b) How does it compare, in construction, with the loose sentence?

6. (a) What are figures? What causes led to their use in language?
   (b) Distinguish between the metaphor and the simile, and give an example of each.
   (c) Which of the two—metaphor or simile—is the more effective?
   (d) Define epigram, synecdoche, apostrophe, irony, and sarcasm.
7. (a) Name some of the special properties of style.
   (b) Distinguish between wit and humor.
8. (a) What is rhythm? Upon what does it depend?
   (b) Define rhyme, verse, stanza, foot, and quatrain.
9. (a) What is the name of the English heroic verse?
   (c) Give the scheme of each of the following kinds of verse: iambic dimeter, trochaic tetrameter and dactylic hexameter.
10. (a) Define poetry.
    (b) The different kinds of poetry may be included under what heads?
    (c) What are the chief qualities of an epic poem?
    (d) Name the so-called *unities* of the drama.
11. (a) Name the chief varieties of prose composition.
    (b) Can you draw a distinction between the novel and the romance?
    (c) Between the sermon and the lecture?
12. (a) Define the essay.
    (b) What are the main divisions of an essay?
    (c) What two forms may the peroration of an essay assume?
    (e) Name two popular American essayists.

EXAMINATION XX.

1. Name three historical events that influenced the early history of the English language.
2. State three principles of paragraphing.

3. (a) What are the rhetorical *qualities* of a sentence?
   (b) Give the rhetorical *classification* of sentences.
4. (a) Give the origin of figures of speech, and their uses.
   (b) Define and illustrate by example, metaphor, apostrophe and euphemism.
5. Scan,—"For the sunset of life gives me mystical lore,
   And coming events cast their shadows before."
6. (a) Discuss title, subject, theme.
   (b) What are the parts of a composition?
   (c) What are the qualities of an introduction?
7. What is poetry? Name four kinds with example to illustrate each.
8. What is syllogism? Illustrate by example.
9. Outline a subject by the *deductive* method, and write on it a short composition, observing all principles of writing.
10. Who wrote "Marcella," "Scarlet Letter," "Ships That Pass in the Night," "Hyperion," "The Alhambra," "Over the Teacups."

3. LATIN.

Sufficient for the Introduction of Cæsar.

LATIN.

EXAMINATION I.

1. How is the declension of a noun determined? How the conjugation of a verb? Illustrate.
2. Decline filia, miles, dies and multus.
3. Compare bonus, acer, similis and altus.
4. Decline ego, is and qui.
5. Write the synopsis of *sum* in the indicative mood; of *pugno* in the subjunctive passive. Conjugate *rego* in the perfect and imperfect subjunctive active.
6. Translate the following:—
   1. Minervae fuit statua magna et clara.
   2. Postero die castra ex eo loco movent.
   3. Eos vincere difficile est, qui nihil timent.
   4. Urbes illae, quarum gloria magna est, a militibus nostris expugunatae sunt.

EXAMINATION II.

1. How do you distinguish the declensions? Illustrate.
2. Write the comparative and superlative of *magnus* and *liber*. Indicate the declension of each in the three genders.
3. Write a synopsis of the verb *porto* in the indicative, active, third, singular; *habeo* in the subjunctive, passive, first, plural; *rego* in the imperative, active, singular; *facio*, infinitives and participles (both forms).
4. Translate:
   (a) Verba bona discipuli a magistro laudabantur.
   (b) Tyranni a viris fortibus contempti sunt.
   (c) Pensum tuum facillimum, meum difficillium est.

5. Translate:
(a) In summer the trees are clothed with leaves.
(b) To know many things is very useful.
(c) Your task is easier than mine; but mine is not very hard.

EXAMINATION III.

1. Give rules of accent.
2. Write genitive singular and plural of a noun of each declension.
3. What forms are given for the principal parts of a verb?
4. Conjugate a verb of each of the regular conjugations in the passive future indicative.
5. How do you find the present and perfect stems of a verb? Illustrate.
6. How are adjectives regularly compared? Illustrate.
7. Form the adverb from the adjective you use and compare it.
8. What are deponent verbs, and how do you tell to which conjugations they belong?
9. Explain construction of indirect discourse.
10. Translate in two ways: "Seas are deeper than rivers."

EXAMINATION IV.

1. How are the different declensions distinguished?
2. Give the case endings of the several declensions.
3. Decline incola, dea, discipulus, granum, homo, urbs, exercitus, vulnus, dies, altus, similis, duo and ipse.
4. How are adjectives compared? Compare justus, acer, dissimilis, magnus and maledicus.
5. How are several conjunctions distinguished?
6. 1. Give a synopsis of duco in the third plu, active and passive.
   2. Conjugate possum in full.
   3. Give a synopsis in the first singular of fio.

Translate:
1. Spes victoriae milites delectabat.
2. Remus a fratre liberatus est.
3. Curabam, ut praeceptor pueri animum excoleret. Nemo dubitat, quin pater puerum semper bene educasset. Boni discipuli student exerceri in literarum studiis.

Change from English to Latin:
1. The soldiers have called the counsel.
2. The boys are praised by the teacher.
3. Does the shade of the woods delight the poet?

EXAMINATION V.

1. What classes of verbs take the dative?
2. What compound verbs take the dative?
3. What verbs take two accusatives?
4. Name some adjectives that take the ablative.
5. Give rule for sequence of tenses.
6. Translate and parse italicized words: Eo *die*, quo consuerat *intervallo, hostes sequitur*, et milia *passuum* tria ab *eorum* castris castra *ponit*.

EXAMINATION VI.

1. Write the case endings of first declension.
2. Decline gener, arvum, nomen, urbs, mare, exercitus, res.
3. Decline magnus, audax.
4. Compare malus, velox, gravis, superus.
5. Compare bene, fortiter, late.
6. Decline is, ille, aliquis, ego.
7. Give characteristic vowel of each conjugation, and conjugate in the perfect tense, indicative and subjunctive mood, active and passive, the following verbs: rogo, doceo, scribo, moneo.
8. Form adverbs from the following adjectives: latus, brevis, facilis, bonus.

9. Translate: Dux imperat ut milites stationes suas servent. Pueri boni a magistro amabuntur et laudabuntur.

10. Change to Latin: The boy was walking with me in the garden yesterday.

EXAMINATION VII.

1. Decline: Mensa, templum, consul, dies, unus and brevior.
2. Conjugate capio.
3. Translate and parse italicized words:
    (a) Nuntiabit Romanos copias Gallorum superavisse.
    (b) Equus *puero* ab agricola *dabatur*.

EXAMINATION VIII.

1. How do we distinguish between the declension of nouns.
2. In how many ways are irregular verbs conjugated and how are they distinguished from each other.
3. Compare the adjective *altus* in all the genders and degrees in the accusative singular.
4. What is the usual order of arranging the Latin sentence.
5. Translate the following and parse underscored words.
    (a) Italia *liberata est*.
    (b) Phillippus *rex* Macedonia, Athenienses superavit.
    (c) Servius Tullius regnavit *annos* quattuor et quadraginta.

EXAMINATION IX.

1. First—How is the declension of a noun determined? Second—Illustrate with a noun in each declension.
2. Give characteristics of each of the four conjugations.
3. Give synopsis of *sum*. Give synopsis of *amo* in the passive voice.
4. Compare *altus, bonus*.
5. Translate and parse nouns, adjectives and verbs in the following sentences: First—Vir duos filios habet.

Second—Caesar jussit milites castra munire. Third—Capella stans in tecto domus, lupum vidit, praetere, euntem, et ludificavit. Sed lupus, "Non tu," inquit, "sed locus tuus, me ludificat."

EXAMINATION X

1. Decline "*vir bonus*," "*puella felix*," and "*bellum civile.*"
2. Compare "*bonus*," "*malus*," "*parvus*," "*multus*," "*magnus*," and "*dives*."
3. Give the tenses in the subjunctive mood of the verb "*eo.*"
4. Give the tenses of the indicative mood, passive voice, of the verb "*rego.*"
5. Translate into English, and construe, "*Dicere pauca, est proprium sapientis.*"
6. Translate into Latin, and construe, "*Labor is useful for the body.*"

EXAMINATION XI.

1. Decline, *ager*, *fertilis*, *sui* and *ille*.
2. (a) Synopsis of sum in the third person singular indicative mood;
   (b) Name and give principal parts of *do* and *gero*.
3. Translate, "*virtus sola, veram voluptatem dat.*"
4. Translate into Latin, "We know that the world is ruled by God."
5. Translate, "*graviter vos accusat quod ab iis sublavetur.*"

EXAMINATION XII.

1. How do you tell the conjugation to which a verb belongs? Illustrate.
2. Decline *amicus*. *Amicitia*.
3. Decline *multus* in the three genders.
4. Write a synopsis of the verb *sum* in the subjunctive moods. *Amo* in the indicative active. Conjugate *moneo* in the perfect subjunctive passive.

5. Translate:
   1. Hi omnes lingua inter se differunt.
   2. Ejus belli haec fuit causa.
   3. His rebus confectis, in Haeduos proficiscitur; civitatem recipit.

EXAMINATION XIII.

1. Translate:
   (1) Undique loci natura Helvetii continentur.
   (2) Summus mons a Tito Labieno tenebatur.
3. Parse *natura* in full.
4. Decline *loci* in the plural.
5. Compare *summus*.
6. What is signified by *ent* and *ur* in the word *continentur*?
7. The verbs in these two sentences have the *same root*, which of them is the derivative word, what change is consequently made in the root, and why?
8. Why is the *preposition omitted* before *natura* and *not* before *Tito*?
9. Translate into Latin: "The tops of the mountains will be held by Caesar."

EXAMINATION XIV.

1. How do you tell the conjugation to which a verb belongs? Illustrate.
2. Decline *amicus*. *Amicitia*.
3. Decline *multus* in the three genders.
4. Write a synopsis of the verb *sum* in the subjunctive mood. *Amo* in the indicative active. Conjugate *moneo* in the perfect subjunctive passive.
5. Translate:
   1. Hi omnes lingua inter se differunt
   2. Ejus belli haec fuit causa.
   3. Erat ex oppido Alesia despectus in campum.

4. ORTHOGRAPHY.

This Branch has in Recent Years Been Very Much Emphasized by the Examiners.

ORTHOGRAPHY.

EXAMINATION I.

1. Nickel.
2. Paregoric.
3. Peaceable.
4. Cancellation.
5. Coercion.
6. Sinister.
7. Soapy.
8. Pheasant.
9. Politician.
10. Emissary.
11. Bilious.
12. Redundant.
13. Resplendent.
14. Victuals.
15. Vitriol.
16. Louisiana.
17. Pharaoh.
18. Vengeance.
19. Volleys.
20. Chancellor.
21. Pigeon.
22. Gluttonous.
23. Sycamore.
24. Magazine.
25. Luscious.
26. Chisel.
27. Arsenic.
28. Hominy.
29. Galaxy.
30. Parasite.
31. Parliament.
32. Delirium.
33. Damageable.
34. Stereotype.
35. Reciprocity.
36. Plaguing.
37. Heinous.
38. Fleece.
39. Crease.
40. Vitrify.
41. Orifice.
42. Ignitible.
43. Scurrility.
44. Serene.
45. Withhold.
46. Woolly.
47. Veneer.
48. Threshold.
49. Satellite.
50. Prodigious.

EXAMINATION II.

1. Omniscient.
2. Deteriorate.
3. Recommend.
4. Surreptitious.
5. Commissary.
6. Auxiliary.
7. Stampede.
8. Antediluvian.
9. Emissary.
10. Assassin.
11. Sterile.
12. Epitome.
13. Inseparable.
14. Nucleus.
15. Excrescence.
16. Taciturn.
17. Oscillate.
18. Restaurant.
19. Resuscitate.
20. Parallelogram.
21. Discernible.
22. Philanthropist.
23. Etiquette.
24. Cohesion.
25. Subtlety.
26. Nonchalance.
27. Authenticity.

ORTHOGRAPHY. 43

28. Aqueous.
29. Pageant.
30. Abscess.
31. Phenomenon.
32. Gorilla.
33. Mercenary.
34. Strychnine.
35. Psychology.

36. Censorious.
37. Acquiescence.
38. Precedent.
39. Embarrass.
40. Farinaceous.
41. Illiterate.
42. Moccasin.
43. Preference.

44. Millionaire.
45. Symphony.
46. Heliotrope.
47. Susceptible.
48. Receptacle.
49. Aggregate.
50. Aquiline.

EXAMINATION III.

1. Prejudice.
2. Malicious.
3. Pewter.
4. Allege.
5. Exonerate.
6. Hypocrisy.
7. Mineralogy.
8. Dentifrice.
9. Stereotype.
10. Apparent.
11. Vitiate.
12. Iodine.
13. Porcelain.
14. Mahogany.
15. Prothonotary.
16. Conferree.
17. Pursuant.

18. Propitious.
19. Suspense.
20. Deficit.
21. Monotonous.
22. Habiliment.
23. Irrevocable.
24. Trisyllable.
25. Artifice.
26. Transparent.
27. Comedian.
28. Mediterranean.
29. Cement.
30. Cochineal.
31. Rhubarb.
32. Dormitory.
33. Buzzard.

34. Conscientious.
35. Immense.
36. Oblige.
37. Anomalous.
38. Equable.
39. Maritime.
40. Orifice.
41. Surplice.
42. Apparel.
43. Monotone.
44. Anodyne.
45. Chicago.
46. Nankeen.
47. Adjacent.
48. Invigorate.
49. Lizard.

EXAMINATION IV.

1. Knoll.
2. Rhinoceros.
3. Enthusiasm.
4. Nauseous.
5. Criticise.
6. Miscellaneous.
7. Complimentary

8. Necessary.
9. Hallelujah.
10. Reservoir.
11. Antiquity.
12. Colleague.
13. Paralysis.
14. Bronchitis.

15. Celery.
16. Kernel.
17. Capitol.
18. Icicle.
19. Presence.
20. Arthur.
21. Richelieu.

22. Hippopotamus.
23. Victuals.
24. Analysis.
25. Pedagogue.
26. Rehearsal.
27. Panegyrics.
28. Physique.
29. Valise.
30. Bouquet.
31. Chronometer.
32. Louisiana.
33. Singeing.
34. Erysipelas.
35. Salary.
36. Tortoise.
37. Plaid.
38. League.
39. Vehicle.
40. Panorama.
41. Reveille.
42. Anxiety.
43. Sergeant.
44. Ridiculous.
45. Typical.
46. Restaurant.
47. Souchong.
48. Christian.
49. Concurrence.
50. Consanguinity.
51. Conceit.
52. Syringe.
53. Pneumonia.
54. Colonel.
55. Capital.
56. Enormous.
57. Cynical.
58. Author.

EXAMINATION V.

1. Nucleus.
2. Coverlet.
3. Coercion.
4. Imminent.
5. Defendant.
6. Cutaneous.
7. Corroborate.
8. Colorado.
9. Palliate.
10. Perforate.
11. Plebeian.
12. Parable.
13. Perceptible.
14. Secession.
15. Arithmetic.
16. Consonance.
17. Chocolate.
18. Bolster.
19. Counterpane.
20. Immerse.
21. Repellent.
22. Antecedent.
23. Disciple.
24. Sedative.
25. Chautauqua.
26. Paralyze.
27. Panacea.
28. Sanitary.
29. Parallel.
30. Promissory.
31. Concession.
32. Preparation.
33. Penurious.
34. Trisyllable.
35. Despair.
36. Collision.
37. Dependent.
38. Descendant.
39. Sustenance.
40. Lenient.
41. Chameleon.
42. Icicle.
43. Propitious.
44. Possessor.
45. Peaceable.
46. Precipice.
47. Procedure.
48. Peremptory.
49. Proselyte.
50. Impurity.

EXAMINATION VI.

1. Tranquillity.
2. Harangue.
3. Scientific.
4. Essential.
5. Subtile.
6. Pedagogic.

ORTHOGRAPHY.

7. Paradise.
8. Descriptions.
9. Discussions.
10. Eschews.
11. Incredulously.
12. Hindoostanee.
13. Aqueous.
14. Ecstasy.
15. Heidelberg.
16. Trophies.
17. Embroidered.
18. Philosophical.
19. Peculiarity.

20. Solicitous.
21. Castile.
22. Consciousness.
23. Delicious.
24. Characteristic.
25. Artificial.
26. Thames.
27. Pyramid.
28. Appreciated.
29. Crypt.
30. Fatiguing.
31. Disease.

32. Conferred.
33. Discipline.
34. Technical.
35. Chapel.
36. Hagiographer.
37. Reconnoitre.
38. Scenery.
39.' Facetious.
40. Symptoms.
41. Lagoons.
42. Mediterranean.
43. Portuguese.

EXAMINATION VII.

1. Sustain.
2. Interval.
3. Subjugate.
4. Real.
5. Gayety.
6. Essence.
7. Quinsy.
8. Palatable.
9. Satellite.
10. Invincible.
11. Dramatize.
12. Diligence.
13. Tingeing.
14. Censorious.
15. Omniscient.
16. Abusable.
17. Punctilious.
18. Abyssinia.
19. Whizzing.
20. Allegeable.

21. Replenish.
22. Tradition.
23. Acrolite.
24. Filially.
25. Nonplus.
26. Utility.
27. Manacle.
28. Supersede.
29. Impanel.
30. Pleiades.
31. Ineligible.
32. Antidote.
33. Unforeseen.
34. Emissary.
35. Glueyness.
36. Immigrant.
37. Infallible.
38. Evangelize.
39. Commissary.
40. Synonymous.

41. Proceed.
42. Benevolent.
43. Accumulate.
44. Cinders.
45. Bilious.
46. Cipher.
47. Ferriage.
48. Extirpate.
49. Derogate.
50. Infringement.
51. Whinny.
52. Italicize.
53. Abridgment.
54. Intelligible.
55. Befitting.
56. Criticise.
57. Judgment.
58. Reversible.
59. Apostrophe.
60. Anglicize.

EXAMINATION VIII.

1. Eyeing.
2. Opacity.
3. Existence.
4. Correlate.
5. Dissertation.
6. Ingenious.
7. Squirrel.
8. Opportunity.
9. Seize.
10. Propagate.
11. Imagine.
12. Defensible.
13. Britannia.
14. Interchangeable
15. Inferring.
16. Preceding.
17. Procedure.
18. Niece.
19. Mackerel.
20. Siege.
21. Carribean.
22. Eel.
23. Exhilaration.
24. Hating.
25. Inconsistency.
26. Indispensable.
27. Analogous.
28. Equivalence.
29. Philip.
30. Sapphire.
31. Flippancy.
32. Hypocrisy
33. Fain.

EXAMINATION IX.

1. Lief.
2. Accordion.
3. Believing.
4. Conscientious.
5. Unconscionable
6. Syncope.
7. Effacement.
8. Sovereignty.
9. Principal.
10. Concealing.
11. Tuesday.
12. Million.
13. Christmas.
14. Beer.
15. Gauge.
16. Sieve.
17. Eclat.
18. Apprehensible.
19. Leaf.
20. Inseparable.
21. Conceit.
22. Recipe.
23. Metaphysical.
24. Granary.
25. Principle.
26. Indelible.
27. Macaulay.
28. Vermilion.
29. February.
30. Bier.
31. Humboldt.
32. Rear.
33. Rice.
34. Conscious.
35. Leaving.
36. Melodeon.
37. Conceive.
38. Receipt.
39. Intelligibly.
40. Tenon.
41. Pristine.
42. Deleble.
43. Rarefy.
44. Rhythm.
45. Wednesday.
46. Clairvoyance.
47. Phidias.
48. Leer.
49. Rise.
50. Stupefy.

1. Write two primitive words, and form derivatives from them.

2. How does a compound word differ from a derivative? Illustrate.

3. Classify the letters according to the organs required to produce the sounds represented by them.
4. How does syncope differ from aphaeresis?
5. What is the object of learning to spell?

EXAMINATION X.

1. Embellish.
2. Aristocracy.
3. Duteous.
4. Bayonet.
5. Parishioner.
6. Moneys.
7. Dulcimer.
8. Isinglass.
9. Hazardous.
10. Prothonotary.
11. Bonfire.
12. Mysterious.
13. Knobby.
14. Recommend.
15. Trafficked.
16. Tragedienne.
17. Gamy.
18. Separate.
19. Nutritious.
20. Tension.
21. Irrefragable.
22. Until.
23. Virtually.
24. Eligible.
25. Euroclydon.
26. Intelligent.
27. Tremendous.
28. Sinecure.
29. Knoll.
30. Italicize.
31. Fac-simile.
32. Tremulous.
33. Towpath.
34. Coalition.
35. Privilege.
36. Beauteous.
37. Syntactical.
38. Pewter.
39. Reciprocity.
40. Deferred.
41. Using.
42. Detrimental.
43. Allopathy.
44. Solstitial.
45. Reprehensible.
46. Nocturnal.
47. Isosceles.
48. Movable.
49. Tragedian.
50. Terrace.

EXAMINATION XI.

1. Metonymy.
2. Arrangement.
3. Repartee.
4. Panegyric.
5. Necessities.
6. Transferring.
7. Decease.
8. Declension.
9. Defamation.
10. Deficit.
11. Deleterious.
12. Demagogue.
13. Domicile.
14. Eligible.
15. Facet.
16. Indelible.
17. Salable.
18. Brilliancy.
19. Aesthetics.
20. Mediaeval.
21. Adamantine.
22. Asphyxia.
23. Altering.
24. Deceit.
25. Decrease.
26. Deference.
27. Defunct.
28. Delicacy.
29. Demonstrable.
30. Dyeing.
31. Emanate.
32. Fascinate.
33. Inseparable.
34. Peaceable.
35. Pretentious.
36. Legitimate.

37. Reference.
38. Connubial.
39. Offering.
40. Decalogue.
41. Decimal.
42. Defalcation.
43. Deficiency.
44. Deign.
45. Delicious.
46. Dense.
47. Duteous.
48. Exhilarate.
49. Financial.
50. Inferrible.

EXAMINATION XII.

1. Amenable.
2. Adventitious.
3. Brevier.
4. Chimerical.
5. Dolomite.
6. Pellicle.
7. Millionaire.
8. Epicene.
9. Pistillate.
10. Scintillate.
11. Subpoena.
12. Precocity.
13. Facetiously.
14. Vaccinate.
15. Pageantry.
16. Guerrilla.
17. Videlicet.
18. Affiliate.
19. Bissextile.
20. Capillary.
21. Corrigible.
22. Anaesthetic.
23. Obsequies.
24. Phylactery.
25. Incineration.
26. Deleble.
27. Smokiness.
28. Syndicate.
29. Hypothecate.
30. Cynosure.
31. Scurrilous.
32. Isosceles.
33. Vacillate.
34. Statistical.
35. Aqueduct.
36. Beneficiary.
37. Catafalque.
38. Doughty.
39. Lacerate.
40. Nauseous.
41. Incendiary.
42. Distractible.
43. Pedagogy.
44. Diligence.
45. Coercion.
46. Gelatine.
47. Indigenous.
48. Monetary.
49. Ingenuous.
50. Reminiscence.

EXAMINATION XIII.

1. Acoustics.
2. Athenaeum.
3. Barouche.
4. Bronchitis.
5. Carbonaceous.
6. Christianity.
7. Cuirass.
8. Diphtheria.
9. Facile.
10. Frankincense.
11. Herbaceous.
12. Inveigle.
13. Mantua-maker.
14. Mnemonics.
15. Phaeton.
16. Spermaceti.
17. Aerolite.
18. Attache.
19. Beethoven.
20. Camelopard.
21. Cerement.
22. Complaisance.
23. Dahlia.
24. Eleemosynary.
25. Falcon.
26. Fratricide.
27. Hypocrisy.
28. Jaguar.
29. Mediocre.
30. Oleomargarine.
31. Pompeii.
32. Finale.
33. Alpaca.

ORTHOGRAPHY. 49

34. Aurora-borealis.
35. Bombazine.
36. Canaanite.
37. Chimpanzee.
38. Conduit.
39. Desuetude.
40. Erysipelas.
41. Flageolet.
42. Guillotine.
43. Insatiable.
44. Kangaroo.
45. Meningitis.
46. Onyx.
47. Raspberry.

EXAMINATION XIV.

1. Kindling.
2. Scissors.
3. Dairy.
4. Spading.
5. Village.
6. Commencement
7. Grammar.
8. Whispering.
9. Lameness.
10. Relax.
11. Glisten.
12. Weevil.
13. Baptize.
14. Melon.
15. Cipher.
16. License.
17. Satchel.
18. Furnace.
19. Pillows.
20. Meadow.
21. Skimming.
22. Sleighing.
23. Graduate.
24. Crayon.
25. Spelling.
26. Ragged.
27. Dandruff.
28. Converge.
29. Onion.
30. Cabbage.
31. Essence.
32. Quotient.
33. Tonnage.
34. Cynical.
35. Cistern.
36. Bureau.
37. Scythe.
38. Rambling.
39. Vacation.
40. Diligent.
41. Pencil.
42. Patient.
43. Ratan.
44. Relapse.
45. Law-suit.
46. Flannel.
47. Anxious.
48. Catarrh.
49. Assessor.
50. Cashier.

EXAMINATION XV.

1. Write a word in which *y* is a *vowel*; one in which it is a *consonant*; one containig a proper diphthong, and one containing an improper triphthong.

2. Classify the consonants according to the organs principally used in producing their sounds, mentioning which consonants belong to each class.

3. Write a list of cognates. Why are they so-called?

4. How is the *d* in stopped pronounced? Why?

5. In what respect is the English alphabet defective?

6. How many different letters and digraphs represent the sound of *a* in *ate*?

7. Write two derivative words in which the spelling of the primitive undergoes change, and defend the change.

8. Write two rules of spelling and illustrate each with two examples.

9. Mark the accent in peremptory, communist, comparable, confidant.

10. Spell, and define all after the seventh.

1. Believe.	8. Siege.	15. Seize.
2. Genitive.	9. Indicative.	16. Infinitive.
3. Imperative.	10. Wean.	17. Ween.
4. Mean.	11. Mien.	18. Right.
5. Rite.	12. Wright.	19. Write.
6. Seen.	13. Scene.	20. Seine.
7. Lief.	14. Leaf.	

EXAMINATION XIV.

1. College.	18. Scholar.	35. Operation.
2. Apportion.	19. Paid.	36. Rhetoric.
3. Foreigner.	20. Indelible.	37. Copy.
4. Edge.	21. Agriculture.	38. Government.
5. Excel.	22. Science.	39. Political.
6. Senior.	23. Musical.	40. Junior.
7. Immense.	24. Grievance.	41. Balance.
8. Believe.	25. Reception.	42. Resemblance.
9. Receive.	26. Procedure.	43. Proceeding.
10. Academy.	27. Monarchy.	44. Providential.
11. Majority.	28. Concerning.	45. Decision.
12. Session.	29. Compulsion.	46. Retention.
13. Coercion.	30. Proper.	47. Common.
14. Recite.	31. Recitation.	48. Philosophy.
15. Oblige.	32. Citizen.	49. Rehearse.
16. Coerce.	33. Reverse.	50. Chorus.
17. Beautiful.	34. Telephone.	

ORTHOGRAPHY. 51

EXAMINATION XVII.

1. Analyze.
2. Benjamin.
3. Conceive.
4. Camphor.
5. Edible.
6. Cincinnati.
7. Geranium.
8. Hosiery.
9. Jehovah.
10. Leisure.
11. Milwaukee.
12. Separation.
13. Surfeit.
14. Thievish.
15. Worcester.
16. Terre Haute.
17. Colorado.
18. Wainscot.
19. Vicinity.
20. Codicil.
21. Utensil.
22. Valet.
23. Turbine.
24. Tumor.
25. Tassel.
26. Surname.
27. Squalid.
28. Sacrilege.
29. Privilege.
30. Nutritious.
31. Respite.
32. Sacrament.
33. Obsolete.
34. Negotiate.
35. Officiate.
36. Abstemious.
37. Madeira.
38. Maintenance.
39. Appurtenance.
40. Prothonotary.
41. Iodine.
42. Inure.
43. Initiate.
44. Indecorous.
45. Herculean.
46. Heliotrope.
47. Homogeneous.
48. Spontaneous.
49. Cutaneous.
50. Surreptitious.

5. READING.

The Course in this Includes, Besides Plain Reading, the Principles of Elocution and Daily Practice in Their Application. The Examination is Generally Oral.

READING.

EXAMINATION I.
1. Upon what should most stress be laid in reading?
2. How should a lesson be assigned?
3. Name some of the qualities of the voice.
4. How much would you assign for a lesson in reading? What should govern the length of a lesson? Should the object of the lesson have anything to do with the length?
5. Would you give pupils extracts to commit to memory? Why?
6. Does the tone of voice in which a word is uttered, have anything to do with its meaning?
7. What is inflection? What determines the inflection of a word or sentence?
8. Name the kinds of emphasis. What determines the kind of emphasis to be employed? What the place?
9. What is articulation? What its importance?
10. What determines the tone of voice with which a piece should be read?

EXAMINATION II.
1. What is articulation, pronunciation, emphasis, gesture, inflection?
2. Tell five ways in which you can determine where to place the emphasis.
3. Tell ten things you would do in conducting a reading lesson.
4. Mark the vowels in the following: look, true, hand, bath, can, can't, master, glass, path, fall, command, one, last, sausage, and, psalm, day, father, knight and prefer.

5. How does the study of elocution aid you in conversation; five ways?
6. Describe the gesture in the following:
    (a) Give thy children food, O, Father!
    (b) We crown her the land of a hundred years.
    (c) The war is inevitable.
    (d) I give thee in thy teeth the lie.
    (e) One vast realm of wonder spreads around.
    (f) May the blessing of heaven rest upon thee.
    (g) Avaunt and quit my sight.
    (h) Be still, sad heart.
    (i) Come let me clutch thee.
    (j) There stands the cottage in which I was born.
7. Mark the inflections in the following:
    (a) To be or not to be, that is the question.
    (b) Speak the speech I pray you as I pronounced it to you.
    (c) Floy, did I ever see Mamma?
8. Mark the emphatic words.
    (a) I said an elder soldier not a better.
    (b) "True I have married her."
    (c) May I have this or that one?
    (d) How old are you, friend?
    (e) The charge is utterly, totally and meanly false.
    (f) "To be or not to be."
    (g) "I think thy brother's soul's in hell to-day.
9. Name the voice in which the following should be read.
    (a) "Live or die, sink or swim, I give my hand and my heart to this vote."
    (b) "I am thy father's spirit."
    (c) "What is so rare as a day in June."
    (d) "To bed, to bed, they're knocking at the gate."
    (e) "I'll have my bond, I'll not hear thee speak."

EXAMINATION III.

1. Write a short article on the subject of "reading," stating the meaning of the term, the object of the study, its value, and the characteristics of *good* reading.

2. Define "inflection."

3. Compare the meanings conveyed by *rising* and *falling* inflections.

4. What is meant by "conception of thought" and how is it obtained?

5. Define time and its elements, and state what kinds of thought are expressed by *slow* and what by *rapid* rate.

6. Underscore the emphatic words in the following:
  (a) "Prosperity is the blessing of the Old Testament; adversity is the blessing of the New."
  (b) "Whoso sheddeth man's blood, by man shall his blood be shed."
  (c) "The man who seeks one thing in life, and but one, may hope to achieve it before life is done; but he who seeks all things wherever he goes, only reaps from the hopes which around him he sows, a harvest of barren regrets."

7. Name the three classes into which English sounds are divided, and define each.

8. Arrange all the elementary sounds according to this classification.

9. Write the table of cognates.

10. Analyze: orchestra, imagery, excursion, trio, finance, truths, courteous, isothermal, hospitable, banquet.

EXAMINATION IV.

1. What do you mean by Messrs.? What is the full word?

2. In the selection you read explain the meaning of "the thunder of the Lord?" Who wrote this? What do you know of him?

3. Why do you emphasize certain words? What do you

mean by emphasis? Name the kinds of emphasis? State when each should be used.

4. In *inquiry*, on which syllable is the accent? In *thanksgiving*? Why are certain expressions placed within dashes? What can you say of the writings of Donald G. Mitchell?

5. What is the title of this piece? (Rip Van Winkle). Who was he? Who wrote this? What is the meaning of "lording it over another?"

6. Which do you consider the more important silent or audible reading—getting the thought or giving it?

7. How can you tell when a piece has been well read?

8. How do you pronounce *Africa?* Give sound of last letter. Write the word upon the blackboard and mark its vowel sounds.

9. In reading poetry do you pay attention to rhyme? State the difference between emphasis and accent. How do you pronounce *inexhaustible*?

10. How do you tell when to keep up your voice in reading and when to let it fall? Are punctuation marks a guide for the voice in reading? Would you always keep up your voice at a comma? How at a semi-colon?

11. How can you tell what words to emphasize? When a word occurs several times in a sentence or in a paragraph, and it has once been emphasized, should it be emphasized again?

12. How many different sounds has *o* ? How does the sound of *o* in *son* differ from that in *some* ?

13. Are there different ways of sounding *th?* Is there a difference in the sound of *th* in *the* and in *thine?*

EXAMINATION V.

"This is the forest primeval. The murmuring pines and the hemlocks,
Bearded with moss, and in garments green, indistinct in the twilight,
Stand like Druids of old with voices sad and pathetic
Stand like harpers hoar, with beards that rest on their bosoms.
Loud from its rocky caverns, the deep-voiced neighboring ocean
Speaks, and in accents disconsolate answers the wail of the forest."

1. Name the quality of voice, the pitch and the rate required in reading the above.
2. What pauses are required in reading poetry that are not required in reading prose?
3. Of what use to the reader are marks of punctuation?
4. Explain what is meant by "murmuring pines," "*bearded* with moss,""Druids,"" eld,"" voices,"" accents," " the wail of the forest," "hemlocks".
5. What words show that pines are old? Why are they compared to harpers?

6. SCHOOL MANAGEMENT.

This Department Includes all that is Commonly Comprised in the Term School Economy; Namely, Organization, Employment and Government.

SCHOOL MANAGEMENT.

EXAMINATION I.

1. Distinguish between method and principle of teaching.
2. What powers are chiefly exercised in the study of reading? of spelling? of arithmetic? of grammar? of drawing?
3. What is reading? Does your answer serve a guide to the method that should be pursued by the teacher?
4. When would you introduce, and to what extent would you carry, elocutionary exercises in connection with reading?
5. Should reviews in teaching be systematically provided for, or be entirely variable in frequency and extent?
6. What is the educational value of manual training?
7. For what purposes will you employ calisthenics?
8. May morning and afternoon recess ever be omitted? if so, when?
9. Specify, in the order of importance, the apparatus that should be provided.
10. Name, including books of reference, the first ten books that should be found in a school library.

EXAMINATION II.

1. If your school room needs ventilation, how will you ventilate it during school hours?
2. What advantages are gained by the teacher from visitation of parents of pupils?
3. What are some abuses likely to arise in a system of graded schools?

NOTE—This list was headed "Methods and School Management."

EXAMINATION III.

1. What branches should be taught in a primary school?
2. What is the place of oral instruction and what that of text books in the primary school?
3. What principles should govern the administration of rewards and punishments in a school?
4. How would you commence to teach geography?
5. What is study as distinguished from the mere preparation of lessons to be recited?
6. Are you in favor of a law compelling children to attend school? Give reasons.

EXAMINATION IV.

1. Define school management.
2. Name chief points in erection of school houses.
3. Give the size and proportion of a building for fifty pupils.
4. What belong to the internal arrangements of a school.
5. What does school hygiene include.
6. Give five important suggestions on school hygiene.
7. Would you recommend close or loose classification? Why?
8. Give plan for opening exercises of school.
9. What are the objects of study?
10. What are the conditions for successful study?

EXAMINATION V.

1. Discuss the location of school houses.
2. What attention should the teacher give to the hygienic habits of the pupils?
3. State the characteristics of good text-books.
4. What are the advantages of a good school program?
5. What are the objects of study?
6. Name six wise incentives to study.
7. State how to secure and hold the attention of pupils.

8. Name and define two methods of recitation.
9. What preparation does the teacher need for the recitation?

EXAMINATION VI.

1. State appropriation: Basis of distribution. When and how paid. How forfeited.
2. Books: Annual selection of—Can be changed—Scriptures a text-book—Sectarian books excluded—Directors not to furnish supplies of—May be purchased by boards.
3. Certificates: Kinds—How obtained?
4. County Superintendent: How elected? Who eligible? Compensation how fixed? Duties of?
5. Directors: How elected and term? Who eligible? Their powers and duties?
6. Houses: How and where erected? Care, control and use of?
7. Institute: County—Schools to be closed?
8. Libraries: How established? Who can use? Property of whom?
9. Normal Schools: Districts. Trustees. Examination of graduates. Certificates of.
10. State Superintendent: Duties of. Appointment. Term of office. Removal.

NOTE—This list was headed "School Law."

EXAMINATION VII.

1. What should be taught in a primary school, and why?
2. Is it just to compel a citizen who has no children to pay taxes to support schools; and if so, on what grounds?
3. Give a list of proper incentives to study.
4. How may the method of learning from nature differ from the methods of learning from text-books?
5. Give an example of the Socratic method of imparting instruction.

6. What is the difference between proving knowledge and testing knowledge?

7. What principle should govern the administration of rewards and punishments in a school?

EXAMINATION VIII.

1. Give a brief synopsis of the School Law of Pennsylvania.

2. Describe what you deem a first-class *school house*, with its grounds, furniture and apparatus.

3. Give your views upon the subject of *school ethics*.

4. Define the school-time of life, and the order of instruction adapted to its various periods.

5. Give a proper course of instruction in primary grammar.

6. What do you understand by the mental, vocal, and physical elements in reading?

EXAMINATION IX.

1. Why do teachers allow school children to play?

2. Define the term "cramming," and give your objections to it, if you have any.

3. How can you secure good manners, and a good moral tone in your school?

4. What purpose have you in view as a teacher?

5. How can you form the habit of quick and thoughtful observation of surrounding phenomena?

EXAMINATION X.

1. School house.
2. School organization.
3. School government.
4. School work.
5. School law: (a) term; (b) school age; (c) teachers' certificates; (d) resources.

EXAMINATION XI.

1. Name five general principles that govern methods.

2. What is the difference between teaching and hearing recitations?

3. What is drill, and when is it not desirable?
4. Is answering in concert ever useful? If so, when?
5. What objects should be attained in teaching geography?
6. Should the teacher in beginning the subject go upon the presumption that the pupil has no geographical knowledge?
7. Can too much map drawing be required? What is the object of it?
8. What considerations should be regarded in determining the size of a lot for a school?
9. How will you ventilate an ordinary school room without injury to the health of the children?
10. What is the proper temperature for a school room?
NOTE—This list was headed "Methods and School Economy."

EXAMINATION XII.

1. State the object of the recitation.
2. Give the proper incentives to study.
3. School administration with reference to offenders.

EXAMINATION XIII.

1. Program for primary school.
2. Various methods to get the parents interested in the school.
3. Improper incentives to study. (Reasons)
4. Weakest points in a free school system.

EXAMINATION XIV.

1. Give a brief analysis of the *Pennsylvania School Law*.
2. Give an outline for the *temporary* and *permanent organization* of the school.
3. What constitutes the *legitimate employments* of the school?
4. State what your views are in reference to the *government* of the school.

7. GEOGRAPHY.

Political, Mathematical, and Physical as a Separate Study.

GEOGRAPHY.

EXAMINATION I.

1. Define the different divisions of geography.
2. Name two of the principal exports of Italy, France, Switzerland, Germany.
3. Locate the following: (a) Samoan Islands; (b) Bermuda Islands; (c) St. Helena; (d) Hawaii; (e) Tasmania.
4. On what waters would a vessel travel in going from Erie, Pa., to Vienna?
5. Draw a map of Pennsylvania, locating the principal cities, mountains and rivers.
6. Locate the Suez Canal. Who controls it? (b) Tell of the Panama canal schemes. (c) Of the Nicaragua canal schemes.
7. If the earth were inclined fifteen degrees to the plane of its orbit, how wide would the temperate zones be?
8. Give proofs of the rotundity of the earth.
9. Give reasons why the Sahara is a desert.
10. To which states of the United States would you go for (1) sugar, (2) salt, (3) tobacco, (4) pine lumber, (5) marble, (6) silver, (7) iron ore, (8) copper, (9) cotton, (10) oysters?

EXAMINATION II.

1. What is political geography? What does it include? Name the principal forms of government. What republics in Africa?
2. What is latitude, longitude, a meridian, a meridian circle? Does a degree of latitude vary? Why? Does a

GEOGRAPHY. 67

degree of longitude vary? Why? How many meridians may be drawn through a parallel?

3. By what are the poles, axis, equator, etc., fixed? Explain.

4. The location of the tropics and polar circles are determined by what?

5. Name the countries of the torrid zone. Name the six largest islands in the world in order of size and locate them.

6. Go from Chicago to Okhotsk sea by water, naming all waters passed through.

7. Bound Brazil and tell all you can of its climate, minerals, government, animals and exports.

8. Describe the climate of the Western coast of North America. Why? Name the countries of Europe and give the capital of each.

9. What countries and islands of North America and the West Indies belong to Great Britain?

10. What does United States export to Great Britain? What does Great Britain export to United States?

EXAMINATION III.

1. Define latitude and longtitude. Is a degree of longitude always equal to a degree of latitude? *Why?*

2. Name, define, and give examples of different kinds of government now existing in Europe.

3. Name and describe the three largest rivers in Europe, locating one city on each.

4. Name and locate five principal mountain ranges in Asia.

5. Compare Africa and South America as to shape, surface, climate, rivers, products, animals and people.

6. Beginning at New York, trace out the chief commercial route around the world, naming waters traversed, countries crossed, and principal cities passed.

7. Name and locate five cities west of the Mississippi river.

8. Name and locate the four principal cities of Canada, and state on what water each is located.

9. Name in order from east to west, the states which lie along the northern boundary of the United States, and name an important product of each.

10. Write a description of China, giving attention to the government, inhabitants, climate, products and commerce.

11. Name the races of man and the largest division, and the largest city inhabited by each.

12. What great empire is composed of islands? Name three important facts about it.

13. Locate and state some fact about the following: (a) Cuba; (b) Greece; (c) Bombay; (d) Hong Kong; (e) Madagascar.

Answer ten.

EXAMINATION IV.

1. Name the great circles and principal small circles of the globe, and state their significance.

2 Designate the motions of the earth stating results, and show the positions of the earth in relation to the sun at the initial points of the season.

3. Where and what are the following: Cincinnati, St. Clair, Dubuque, Shasta Hood, San Lucas, Rio Janeiro, Cayenne, Volga, Ceylon, Barcelona and Manilla.

4. State where the following commercial commodities are obtained, principally: tin, copper, iron, coal, salt, gypsum, petroleum, diamonds, ostrich feathers, ivory, opium, tea, coffee, cork, lead, silver and gold.

5. Name recent changes either in the geography or government of any countries of the world.

6. Name geological ages and discuss one.

7. State theories of tides, and give details of theory you regard as most plausible.

8. Name climatic zones and give boundaries.

GEOGRAPHY. 69

EXAMINATION V.

1. In going from this school via Harrisburg and Chicago to San Francisco, over what railroad would you pass and through what states and territorites?
2. Sketch the Mississippi river system; mark approximate latitude.
3. Great Britain: A few leading exports and imports; its foreign possessions.
4. Causes of change of seasons.'
5. Causes of tides, spring and neap.
6. State principal geographical facts you gleaned from newspapers the past year.
7. In going from New York on the most direct commercial route, around the world, name the important ports you would touch.
8. State geographical position and political relations of (1) Cuba, (2) Philippine islands (3) Java, (4) Canaries.

EXAMINATION VI.

1. What are trade winds? Counter trade winds? Explain cause of ocean currents.
2. What season have the Chinese now? The Peruvians? The Hindoo? The Australians? The Patagonians?
3. Locate the principal rainless regions of the world, and give reasons.
4. Give proofs that the industries of a country are controlled by its geography.
5. Contrast the government of the United States with that of China.
6. Name the three leading manufacturing countries of Europe. Which European country is noted for fairs? For fisheries? For marble?

EXAMINATION VII.

1. Draw a representation of the Solar system.
2. Where are the sun's rays vertical when we have our longest day? When? Where are they vertical when the

days and nights are equal? When? When are they vertical with us?

3. What are the general features of continental relief? Draw a cross section of North America.

4. Draw a memory map of South America. Represent the mountains and rivers.

5. Describe the drainage of South America. If the Brazilian mountains extended to the Isthmus of Panama what effect would it have on the drainage of the continent?

6. Name and describe the two main offices of rivers. Give examples.

7. Explain tides, dew and clouds. Trace the Japan current.

8. What are the principal causes which modify temperature? What parts of Europe have the same annual temperature as Alaska? Give cause.

9. In what way are animals and plants dependent on each other.

10. What are the five great races of mankind? In what way is the distribution of labor dependent on Physical Geography?

EXAMINATION VIII.

1. Name the divisions of geography and define each.

2. Define orbit, meridian, solar system and name the planets in order of distance from the sun.

3. Name the geological ages, give characteristic features of each, and name the agencies that still produce changes in the earth's crust.

4. Define plain, plateau and mountain system, and name the plains of Asia, the plateaus of North America and the mountain systems of Europe.

5. Discuss tides, define co-tidal lines and tell why high tide occurs fifty-four minutes later each day.

6. Define ocean currents, give causes, and describe the Gulf stream.

GEOGRAPHY. 71

7. Discuss trade winds and explain the formation of dew.
8. Define atmosphere, climate, and give the conditions upon which climate depends.
9. Classify animals, name the races of mankind, and describe the Aryan division.
10. Account for the following: Lack of rain in Central Asia; mild climate of Northwestern United States; dense fogs of Newfoundland; heavy rainfall in the Amazon valley.

EXAMINATION IX.

1. Explain why our days just now are longer than the nights?
2. Why are the tropics placed where they are?
3. Of what is the air composed? What instrument measures its pressure? What is the weight of the air at sea level?
4. On what four things does climate depend?
5. Name four uses of rivers?
6. Sketch the Mississippi river, showing its four leading branches and the location of four cities.
7. Name six of the most densely populated countries in the world.
8. Name the six great powers of the world.
9. Name four leading cotton countries.
10. What and where: Pamir, Cotopaxi, Nyassa, Cashmere, Astrakan, Novgorod, Seattle, Dardanelles, Copenhagen, Suez, Teneriffe, Vancouver, Tokio.
11. Name six of the principal harbors of the world.

EXAMINATION X.

1. Define the following: orbit, horizon, tropic, meridian.
2. Locate six cities in the New England states (not capitals).
3. Name and locate the principal seaboard cities in the United States.

4. Name the government of France, its rivers and its exports.
5. Name six of the most important cities in Europe. For what are they noted?
6. Climate—The winds.

EXAMINATION XI.

1. Describe six rivers in Pennsylvania.
2. Locate the following and state for what each is noted: Altoona, Knoxville, Corry, Crimea, Como, Quito, Rhine, Minneapolis, Winchester, Leadville, Golden Gate, Thames, Apennines, West Point, Bradford, Milan, Leipsic.
3. Which state is the geographical centre of the United States?
4. Into what divisions may the United States be divided with reference to its drainage?
5. How do the United States and China compare in size and population?
6. Why are the Pacific slopes of Peru and Bolivia rainless?

EXAMINATION XII.

1. What is supposed to be the reason why the earth is flattened at the poles?
2. Name the two great mountain systems of the United States; the four great rivers; the largest four cities; and the three great seaports.
3. Why does so little rain fall on that part of South America west of the Andes mountains?
4. What is the length of the longest day at the equator? on the Arctic circle? at the North pole?
5. Name a large city in Europe noted for the manufacture of cotton cloth? one noted for its silks? one noted for its linen?
6. What part of the United States is a plateau or high-

GEOGRAPHY. 73

land? Why does it have less rain than the valley of the Mississippi?

7. Name the two great rivers of South America; two of Africa; four of Europe.

8. What country produces the most cotton? The most sugar? the most rice? the most coffee?

9. By what two great commercial routes can we travel around the world, starting from New York?

10. Why does the climate of Labrador differ so materially from that of England?

EXAMINATION XIII.

1. Name and describe three of the largest rivers on the earth.

2. Of what states is the empire of Germany composed? Bound it and locate the capital and three other large cities.

3. Describe the physical features of North America. Give its principal mining regions and tell what they produce.

4. Describe the Yukon river.

5. What industries predominate in (a) the New England states? (b) the Gulf states? (c) the Mississippi valley? (d) the Pacific states?

EXAMINATION XIV.

1. What states of the United States are mostly engaged in manufacturing? In farming? In mining? What states produce the most corn, wheat, cotton, rice, sugar?

2. Describe the general arrangement of the great mountain systems and the low plains of Asia.

3. On what waters would you sail in going from Chicago to Sevastopol?

4. State the situation of the following places: St. Louis, Cheyenne, Trebizond, Canton, Manila, Bombay, Edinburg, Mt. Etna, Lake Tchad.

5. Which has at any time the longer day, Para or Christiania? Why?

6. Where is the coffee tree most extensively cultivated? sugar cane? cinnamon? cotton plant?

7. State the characteristics of the temperate fauna, naming the principal carnivora, herbivora, rodentia, cetacea, marsupials and birds.

8. Name the currents of which the atmospheric circulation principally consists, and the causes which produce the shifting of the equatorial and polar currents.

9. Describe the Gulf stream, and state what influence it has on the climate of certain countries.

10. What are monsoons?

EXAMINATION XV.

1. State the width in degrees of the zones. How determined?

2. Why do no longer streams of South America flow in the Pacific ocean.

3. Which is further north, Cincinnati or Rome? England or Newfoundland?

4. State the prevailing directions of the mountainous chains of the continents.

5. Name the five great powers and the form of government in each.

6. Locate and describe Spitzenbergen, St. Helena, New Zealand, Vancouver and Mauritius.

7. In which zone are the most highly civilized nations found. Why?

8. From what countries do we get cloves, nutmegs, platinum, tin, gutta-percha.

9. Does Mercator's map show countries in their true relation? Show why.

10. Name ten seas bordering on Asia.

GEOGRAPHY. 75

EXAMINATION XVI.

1. Distinguish between physical and mathematical geography.
2. Describe the currents of the Pacific ocean. Tell how caused and what benefit results from them.
3. Discuss the various forms of precipitation of moisture.
4. What is the cause of deserts? Illustrate.
5. What is the Darwinian theory of coral island?
6. Name three principal mountain ranges in North America; in Europe; in Asia.
7. Tell the situation of the following cities: Chicago, St. Louis, Detroit, Portland, Havana, Rio Janeiro, Callao, Cairo, Smyrna, Venice and Bombay.
8. What are the principal agencies that have made New York city the commercial metropolis of the United States?
9. Name three centres of population of Europe and tell why they are such.
10. Give an account of African exploration within the past half century.

EXAMINATION XVII.

1. Are the days longer now at Halifax or at Augustine?
2. Where is the longest day one month in length?
3. What are isothermal lines, and why do they differ from parallels?
4. Discuss the northeast trade wind.
5. What relation is there between the vegetation of a country and its forms of relief?
6. Locate all the cities in about the same latitude as New Orleans.
7. Compare Cuba with Newfoundland, mentioning points of likeness and of difference.

EXAMINATION XVIII.

1. Show that the earth's shadow on the moon, and the circumnavigation of the globe prove the earth spherical.

2. What are the tropics, why so called, and how are they determined?

3. Illustrate by diagram the divisions of land distinguished by different relations to adjacent waters, and by differences of elevation.

4. The atmosphere, its composition, weight, heat and moisture.

5. Explain how the movements of the atmosphere are caused and modified, and distinguish between the trades and the anti-trades.

6. In what respect does a tidal wave differ from a wind wave? Explain how each is produced.

7. What effect have surface currents of the ocean upon temperature?

8. What constitutes an *artesian well?* How does it differ from the *intermittent* spring?

9. How does the slope of a country influence its commercial and social life?

10. State the important facts that belong to the geography of the Pacific states of our country.

EXAMINATION XIX.

1. Define the following terms: meridian, promontory, canon, delta, watershed, ecliptic and zone.

2. Bound Italy; name its principal mountains and streams, largest city and principal seaports.

3. Describe the position of the highest mountain system in each of the grand divisions. Give the name, position and altitude of at least one prominent peak in each system.

4. Discuss land and sea breezes.

5. Explain the origin of constant currents and how the rotation of the earth affects the directions of constant currents.

6. Trace a water route from Chicago to Sebastopol.

7. Give the boundaries of the mathematical climatic zones. Name the causes which prevent the mathematical climatic zones from coinciding with the physical climatic zones.

8. Mention the ten largest cities in the United States.

9. Name and describe the central plains of South Amercia.

10. Bound Kentucky. Name six streams and five cities. Discuss its natural features.

EXAMINATION XX.

1. Discuss the theory of air-currents. Of water-currents.

2. What is the theory of rain-fall and its relation to climate?

3. Trace a great trade-route around the world, locate the cities on the route, and give reasons for their position and size.

4. State the causes of the change of seasons. What results would arise if the angle of the inclination of the earth's axis were seventy-five degrees?

5. Describe the representative governments of Europe.

EXAMINATION XXI.

1. Give the motions of the earth and state what they produce.

2. Locate the tropics and polar circles, and give reason why they are so located.

3. Name the continents. Tell the different forms of government and name a country under each form.

4. What importance do you attach to map drawing and moulding?

5. Compare the products of the Northern states with those of the Southern.

6. Name and locate a river system, a mountain system, and a railroad system—the latter to be in the United States.

7. On what does the climate of a country chiefly depend?
8. What is rain, snow, dew?
9. Why do we get our continuous rains from the east?

EXAMINATION XXII.

1. What are the proofs that the earth revolves on its axis.
2. On June 21, what will be the position of the earth in relation to the sun?
3. What caused the earth to become a spheroid?
4. What is the area and population of Pennsylvania, Europe and Cuba?
5. What is the effect of altitude on the amount of rain.
6. Which is the greater distance, 5° north from Shippensburg, or 5° east? Why?
7. Explain the origin of the trade winds.
8. Who owns Elba, Cyprus, Corsica, Madagascar, Porto Rico?
9. What is the cause of earthquakes?

EXAMINATION XXIII.

1. Define meridian, isothermal, snow-line, sirocco, atoll, avalanche.
2. Name the largest four rivers in each of the five grand divisions.
3. Name the principal mountain chains in Asia and Africa, and give reasons for the trend of each.
4. Name the most important country in each of the grand divisions.
5. Locate the following and tell for what each is noted: Moscow, Valladolid, Bombay, Alps, Scranton, Patsco, Utrecht, Augsburg, Timbuctoo, Erie, Chester, Aspinwall, Washington, Pa., Glasgow.
6. Discuss the causes of volcanoes, mineral springs, trade winds, ocean currents.

GEOGRAPHY. 79

7. Name five of the principal articles exported by the people of the United States, also five of the principal articles imported into the United States.

8. Name the political divisions of Asia and South America, also the kingdoms and principalities of Europe.

8. HISTORY OF THE UNITED STATES.

In this Branch Great Thoroughness is Required. A Knowledge of Facts, However, is not Sufficient. The Applicant Must Know Something of the Relation of Events to One Another.

History of the United States.

EXAMINATION I.

1. Name the three classes of Colonial governments existing at the beginning of the Revolution and tell to which class the following colonies belong: New York, Massachusetts, Pennsylvania, Virginia.

2. Upon whose discoveries did the English base their claim to the coast from Newfoundland to Virginia? Upon whose explorations did the Dutch base their claim to the coast from Cape Cod to Delaware bay?

3. Who was President of the United States during the war of 1812? Mexican war? Civil war?

4. Name the states which seceded from the Union.

5. How many states were there at the beginning of the Civil war in 1861? How many at its close in 1865? How many at the present time?

6. Name some of the most noted American historians, poets, authors, editors and orators.

EXAMINATION II.

1. Give a brief account of Columbus and his voyage to America.

2. Name three English explorers and the regions they visited.

3. What was the "Hartford Convention?" The Omnibus bill?

4. Give an account of the Dutch settlements in the New World.

HISTORY OF THE UNITED STATES. 83

5. Who were the six nations? What influence did they have upon the surrounding tribes, and what part did they play in the history of the colonies?

6. What settlement was made of the Alabama claims in 1872?

7. Name four wars of the United States, their causes, the most decisive battle in each, and the men who won greatest renown as warriors or soldiers.

8. What was the original extent and limit of the United States, and how has her present territory increased since?

9. Give a brief account of the following: Hamilton, Arnold, Marquette, Braddock, Oglethorpe, Clay, Benton, Webster, Sumner, Sherman.

10. What were the prominent events of Jefferson's administration? Jackson's? Monroe's? Grant's?

11. Name the leading historical events of the past two years.

EXAMINATION III.

1. For what discoveries are Balboa and Ferdinand-de-Soto noted?

2. Name some events between the close of the Revolutionary war and Washington's administration.

3. Give the cause and result of the Mexican war.

4. Who effected, and what was the Louisiana purchase?

5. What was the Kansas-Nebraska bill?

6. Give facts about Antietam, Fredericksburg and Appomattox.

7. To what cabinet officer is the management of foreign affairs entrusted? Who fills the office under Cleveland's present administration? Under Harrison's administration?

EXAMINATION IV.

1. Where was Lord Baltimore from and what was his purpose in coming to America?

2. Give some facts about Calhoun, Clay, Stanton and Conkling.
3. Under whose administrations did the various wars of the United States occur?
4. Give an account of the admission of Kansas?
5. What is the civil service act and what objections are urged against it.
6. Discuss the Mound Builders.

EXAMINATION V.

1. Who were the Mound Builders and the Northmen?
2. Who were the Jesuit Missionaries, and what did they do?
3. Give the history of the settlement of Pennsylvania.
4. Name all the Colonial wars giving date of beginning.
5. Name the Presidents in their order from 1841 to 1861, giving date of inauguration and party electing.
6. Give the cause of the crisis of 1837.
7. In what way have the public lands often threatened the peace of our country?
8. What were the causes which led to the war with Mexico?
9. Give the history of the Trent affair.
10. What difficulties arose between President Johnson and Congress?

EXAMINATION VI.

1. Mention the three classes of discoveries and explorations, and the territories to which they were confined.
2. Describe the different forms of government existing during the Colonial period. Compare the settlements of Massachusetts, Virginia and New York during Colonial days as regards religion, education and form of government.
3. Give the causes of the "Great Wars" in which our country has been involved. What effect did the French and Indian have upon the colonies?

HISTORY OF THE UNITED STATES. 85

4. Mention the three most decisive battles of the Revolutionary war. Why? Give principal events between close of this war and Washington's administration.

5. Distinguish between a protective tariff and a revenue tariff.

6. What is meant by state rights, constitutional supremacy, the spoils system, civil service reform, inter-state commerce law.

7. Give the history of the United States bank.

8. Give the causes of the financial crises our country has suffered.

9. For what are the following names famous in American history: (a) Robert Morris, (b) Franklin, (c) John Jay, (d) Paul Jones, (e) Hamilton, (f) Sumner, (g) Clay, (h) Washington Irving?

10. Mention the boundary difficulties.

11. Discuss briefly (a) Monroe Doctrine, (b) Kansas-Nebraska Bill, (c) Wilmot Proviso, (d) Alien and Sedition laws.

12. Mention the leading historical events of the last four years.

EXAMINATION VII.

1. Discoveries by the Cabots. Discuss.

2. Write a brief account of early settlement of Pennsylvania.

3. What effect upon the colonies did the French and Indian war have?

4. Name the cause of the war of 1812, and locate the principal engagements on land and sea.

5. What is a protective tariff? Free trade? Civil service?

6. What can you say of the industrial growth and manufacturing interests of the United States?

7. Of what educational value was the Columbian Exposition to the people of the United States?

EXAMINATION VIII.

1. Give proofs that America was discovered prior to the arrival of Columbus?
2. Early settlement of four states—when, where, by whom, from what motives?
3. What was the most important event of Jefferson's administration?
4. How was John Quincy Adams elected President?
5. Discuss these subjects: Tippecanoe, Paul Jones, Brownlow, Valley Forge, Lyons, Wayne, Thomas, 1755, Benton, Slidell, Clay.
6. Write one page on slavery.

EXAMINATION IX.

1. What land did Columbus first discover, and when? How many voyages did he make? What reward did he receive for his discoveries? Where was he buried?
2. What nations explored the future United States? When, and by what nation was negro slavery introduced into the United States?
3. What were the chief causes which led to the American Revolution? What was the Stamp act? Who was Patrick Henry?
4. Describe the attack on Fort Moultrie.
5. When did General Washington take command of the American army, and how large was his force? How did he force the British to evacuate Boston?
6. When was the Declaration of Independence accepted by Congress? What did it declare? What became necessary after this declaration?
7. When, where, and to whom did Burgoyne surrender? What was the agreement in this surrender?
8. Describe the surrender of Detroit during the war of 1812.
9. What were the causes which led to the war with

Mexico? What was the treaty of peace between the United States and Mexico?

10. When, where, and with what result was the encounter between the Kearsarge and the Alabama? How was slavery abolished in the United States?

EXAMINATION X.

1. Give an account of the voyages of John and Sebastian Cabot.

2. Relate what you regard as the more important events connected with the colonization of Massachusetts.

3. Give a brief account of the life and public services of William Penn.

4. When and under what circumstances was Harvard college founded? The printing press introduced into this country?

5. Say what you can about the thirteenth and fourteenth amendments to the constitution.

EXAMINATION XI.

1. What four nations were the early explorers of the United States, and what portion of the continent did each explore?

2. What territory has the United States acquired by purchase? By conquest? By annexation?

3. Define the Kansas-Nebraska Bill; the Dred Scott decision.

4. Name five great men our country has produced. Tell what three of these men have done.

5. Mention two leading events of each of the following administrations: Monroe's, Jackson's, Pierce's.

6. When was the "Emancipation Proclamation" issued, and what was the effect on the nation?

7. What political convention recently met at Indianapolis, and what was done? What one met at Chicago? What was done?

EXAMINATION XII.

1. From what nations have we acquired Louisiana, Florida, California?
2. Name the battles fought and two towns captured by Gen. Taylor in the Mexican war?
3. By whom and for what length of time are senators in Congress elected?
4. What did Count Rochambeau do for the Americans?
5. Why did the colonies think England had no right to tax them?
6. What taxes were imposed immediately after the repeal of the stamp act?
7. What powers are vested in the general government?
8. What exclusive powers have the states?
9. Where must bills for raising revenue originate?
10. How can the constitution be amended?
11. Mention the last amendment.

EXAMINATION XIII.

1. What nations took part in the exploration of North America? Indicate upon a map the sections settled by those most successful in making permanent settlements, and from governments, and in what way we have come in possession of the whole land.
2. Name the wars that have been waged. Which of these noticeably affected our subsequent history? Name one or more effects of the last.
3. Name any other agencies or events, such as inventions, discoveries, or acts of Congress that have affected the current of our history. Name one effect of each.
4. Who was Ben. Franklin? Greene? Alex. Hamilton? Thos. H. Benton? S. J. Tilden? Andrew Jackson? Daniel Webster? Eli Whitney? Thaddeus Stevens? W. S. Hancock? Select five.
5. Where are the following and why celebrated. Acadia,

HISTORY OF THE UNITED STATES. 89

Appomattox Court House, San Salvador, Valley Forge, Fort Donelson?

6. Name five great statesmen, five great writers, five great commanders, three great Presidents, or four if you can.

7. Give topical outline of Monroe's administration.

EXAMINATION XIV.

1. Discuss the explanation made by four principal English explorers.
2. Name and describe the three prevailing forms of government in the original colonies.
3. During what period of time did these forms exist in Virginia?
4. Name the five objective points of the French and Indian war, and why were the English so persistent in their attacks upon them, and the French so obstinate in their resistance?
5. Describe the battle of Long Island.
6. What decided it in favor of the English?
7. What were the Alien and Sedition laws?
8. Why were they passed?
9. How received?
10. Give a topical outline of Monroe's administration.
11. Recite Henry Clay's measures of '50.
12. What noted person was their warmest supporter?
13. Describe the battle between the Monitor and the Merrimac.
14. Give a full discussion of the effect of the contest.
15. Discuss the Alabama claims.
16. What other questions were settled by the same treaty?
17. What great principle of the settlement of disputes was thus established?
18. Name the officers of Harrison's cabinet.

EXAMINATION XV.

1. State where the Cabots made discoveries in America.
2. What were the compromise measures of 1820? Of 1850?
3. When, how, and from whom was the following territory acquired: Florida, Louisiana, California, Alaska?
4. In the history of this country what have been the most important acts of legislation? Why?
5. Name four of the most noted men that have been Secretary of the Treasury, Secretary of State. To what state does each one belong?
6. Give some of the results of the war with Mexico, and show how they have affected the development of our country.

EXAMINATION XVI.

1. Give a brief account of the early history of Pennsylvania.
2. Mention some facts of the customs, schools, money and occupations of the colonists.
3. State the immediate and the remote causes of the American Revolution.
4. Why was the Monroe doctrine passed? What were its provisions.
5. Discuss what is known as "The Kansas Question?"
6. Name the political parties and the candidates of each in the Presidential campaign of 1860.
7. Discuss some current political question.

EXAMINATION XVII.

1. Name five important events of the Colonial period.
2. State the causes that led to the Revolution.
3. Name five battles of the Revolution and their results.
4. Name five noted American generals, five English and five foreign ones who assisted the Americans.
5. Which nation of Europe first recognized the independence of the Americans?

HISTORY OF THE UNITED STATES. 91

6. State the causes of the second war with Great Britain.
7. Name the important battles and the prominent generals of each side.
8. Give a synopsis of the great rebellion.
9. The purchases and acquisitions of territory by the United States.
10. The great American inventions of the nineteenth century.

EXAMINATION XVIII.

1. Give brief sketches of DeSota, John Hancock and Charles Sumner.
2. Settlement and early history of Massachusetts.
3. Give a complete history of Fort DuQuesne.
4. Describe two battles fought at Quebec.
5. State the causes and effects of Burgoyne's surrender.
6. State the leading events of Jackson's administration.
7. Brief description of the battle of Gettysburg.
8. Explain Monroe doctrine and Omnibus bill.

EXAMINATION XIX.

1. Name the cause, time and result of the Mexican and French and Indian wars.
2. What was the Missouri compromise?
3. Explain the Omnibus bill.
4. What is the Monroe doctrine.
5. Give a short account of the first permanent English settlement.
6. When, where and by whom was the first permanent French settlement made?
7. Give a short account of the acquisition of Florida and Alaska.
8. How and when was negro slavery introduced, and how abolished?

EXAMINATION XX.

1. Name four Colonial wars, and one leading event in each.

2. By whom was Louisiana settled, and how did it become a part of the United States?

3. What great battle would not have been fought if the Atlantic cable had been laid soon enough?

4. What aid did France extend to the United States in the war of the Revolution?

5. Where was the last battle of the Revolution fought, and who were the opposing generals?

6. How did the United States obtain Florida, Texas, California and Oregon?

7. Name an English, a Dutch, a Spanish, and an Italian discoverer.

8. Cause of the great rebellion, and what states passed ordinances of secession.

9. CIVIL GOVERNMENT

Constitution of the United States, Some Acquaintance With the State Constitution and a Knowledge of Local Government.

CIVIL GOVERNMENT.

EXAMINATION I.

1. Define civil government, state, citizen, public domain, and reciprocity.
2. Write the preamble to the constitution.
3. Describe two ways in which a bill may become a law.
4. Explain the following: (1) habeas corpus, (2) bill of attainder, (3) ex-post facto law, (4) naturalization.
5. Describe the methods of electing a President, omitting small details.
6. Discuss the Supreme Court of the United States.
7. Give constitutional qualifications, term of office, and salary of Representative, Senator, President, Vice-President and Supreme Judges.
8. Who is chief justice of the Supreme Court of Pennsylvania, and what salary does he receive?
9. What is the number of your Congressional district? Of what counties composed? Who is your Congressman?
10. Who is Superintendent of Public Instruction? What are some of his duties?

EXAMINATION II.

1. Name three forms of government and define each.
2. Give qualification of Representatives, of Senators.
3. Give special duties belonging to Representatives, to Senators.
4. Name five prohibitions of Congress. Define "habeas corpus," "ex-post facto law," "bill of attainder."

CIVIL GOVERNMENT. 95

EXAMINATION III.

1. Brief synopsis of the constitution.
2. Difference between a republic and a pure democracy.
3. How does a territory become a state?
4. How are amendments to the constitution made?
5. How many United States Senators are there?
6. What are the qualifications of a voter in this state.

EXAMINATION IV.

1. Name the public officers of a town or township, and state briefly the duties of each.
2. Give the preamble of the constitution of the United States.
3. What is meant by a writ of habeas corpus?
4. What is required of an author or proprietor in order to obtain a copyright?
5. How are laws enacted by Congress?
6. How are United States Senators elected and what are the requisite qualifications?
7. How is an alien made a citizen of the United States.
8. What are "letters of marque and reprisal."
9. How are the trials of impeachment conducted?
10. How are the number of electors determined to which each state is entitled?

EXAMINATION V.

1. What is a bill; how may it become a law?
2. How are vacancies in the House and Senate filled?
3. What is meant by civil liberty?
4. Define: "ex-post facto law," "bill of attainder."
5. (a) In what is the judicial power of the United States vested?
   (b) How many judges in the Supreme Court?
   (c) Their term of office?
   (d) How appointed?
   (e) Who is present chief justice??
6. Name six powers of Congress.

EXAMINATION VI.

1. How is the President nominated and elected? A Senator? A Circuit Judge?
2. How often does Congress meet? When? Define "a Congress."
3. What is a copyright? A patent? An ex-post facto law? Letters of marque? Reciprocity? Give law concerning, and examples.
4. How may an alien become a naturalized citizen?
5. Explain the succesive proceedings in a criminal case, in a court of quarter sessions.

EXAMINATION VII.

1. How are United States Senators chosen? Explain how the United States Senate is a continuous body. Name two sole powers of the Senate, constitutional qualifications required for the office.
2. Recite the preamble of the constitution of the United States. What is a constitution?
3. State all the steps through which a bill may go before it becomes a law.
4. Name the three departments of our national and state governments, and state the general purpose of each.
5. In case a voter is challenged, what course must he pursue in order to vote?
6. How does a foreigner become a citizen of the United States?
7. What are the titles of the members of the President's cabinet? Name at least five members.
8. Explain in detail how the President of the United States is elected.

EXAMINATION VIII.

1. What influences determined that each state should have, in the lower house of Congress, representation in proportion to its population, while the number in the upper house should always remain the same?

CIVIL GOVERNMENT. 97

2. How are members of the House of Representatives chosen? Name three exclusive powers of this branch of the legislative department.

3. How are United States Senators chosen? Explain how the Senate is a continuous body. Name two sole powers of the Senate.

4. Has the President pro-tem. a right to vote on all measures while he is serving as Vice-President? Why?

5. State all the steps a bill may go through before it becomes a law.

6. How does a foreigner become a citizen of the United States?

7. Name the United States courts. What is the court of claims?

8. In what cases has the United States Supreme Court original jurisdiction? In what appellate?

9. Where is the power to declare war vested in this country?

10. In what two ways may the constitution be amended?

EXAMINATION IX.

1. What is a state?

2. By what authority is the state divided into congressional districts?

3. State three qualifications that a voter at our state elections must have.

4. If an elector own land in several states, can he vote in them all? What facts determine his legal residence?

5. Can a state make a treaty with another state or nation? Give reasons for your answer.

6. (a) What is an extradition treaty? (b) What is an ex-post facto law?

7. What is the right of suffrage? Is it a natural or civil right?

8. Name the three departments of the government, and state briefly the duties of each.

9. It is proposed to elect United States Senators by a direct vote of the people, how must the requisite constitutional change be made?

10. What are consuls? State their duties.

EXAMINATION X.

1. Define government, laws.
2. What is a state? A constitution?
3. Name and define the different classes of Colonial governments.
4. How old must a Representative be? What other qualifications are necessary? How are the vacancies in the representation from any state to be filled?
5. Repeat the clause which relates to revenue bills.
6. Give the different processes by which a bill may become a law.
7. Define habeas corpus, ex-post facto law, bill of attainder.
8. What powers are granted to Congress?
9. Repeat the clause of the constitution which defines the qualifications of the President. What are the powers and duties of the President?
10. Who would be President in case of removal, death, resignation or inability both of the President and Vice-President.
11. Constitutional amendment, how prepared and how ratified.
12. Where is the judicial power of the United States vested?

EXAMINATION XI.

1 Recite the preamble.
2. What is a constitution?
3. Describe the process of naturalization.
4 Explain the terms, members-at-large, electoral college.

5. Show the process by which a vetoed bill may become a law.

6. How are vacancies filled in the House of Representatives and Senate?

EXAMINATION XII.

1. What is a constitution?

2. What are legislative powers, and in what are they vested?

3. How are Senators and Representatives elected? For how long a term of office? How is their number determined?

4. If vacancies happen in the representation of any state, how is the vacancy filled?

5. Who is the President of the Senate? Can he vote?

6. What is impeachment?

7. When shall Congress assemble? Can it assemble at any time? Can a member be arrested while Congress is in session? How do members receive compensation?

8. In whom is the executive power of the United States vested? Who are eligible to this office? How are the President and Vice-President elected?

9. What power has Congress in regard to the territory and other property belonging to the United States?

10. What is the supreme law of the land? Who are bound by oath to support it?

EXAMINATION XIII.

1. How is the President of the United States elected? If the President and Vice-President should resign or be removed from office, who would succeed to the presidency?

2. What bills must originate in the House? Why? In what ways may a bill become a law without the President's signature?

3. How may members of the legislative department be removed? Members of the executive and judicial departments?

EXAMINATION XIV.

1. When was the confederation formed? How long did it last? State its principal defects.

2. How many members are there in the House of Representatives? By whom elected? For what term? How apportioned among the states at first? How apportioned now? Qualifications?

3. Anwer the same question as to the Senate.

4. What is protection? Free trade? State the chief arguments for each. Which is the policy of the United States?

5. What is a bill of attainder? An ex-post facto law? An appropriation by Congress?

6. What are the President's qualifications? Salary? Name the auxiliary executive departments.

7. How did the constitution originally become binding on a state? How does an amendment to it become binding?

8. Are the judges of the Supreme Court of the United States appointed or elected? Of what is the Supreme Court composed? What can you say of compensation?

EXAMINATION XV.

1. Discriminate socialists and anarchists.

2. What rights did Congress gain and the states surrender by the adoption of the constitution?

3. Whence is the money necessary to carry on the government of the United States derived?

4. Justify the creation and existence of the Senate.

5. What officers of the government of the United States are there in a foreign country? To what department do they belong?

EXAMINATION XVI.

1. From what source did the United States government originally derive its authority?

2. Name a few civil and a few political rights.

3. What is meant by the right of eminent domain?
4. Define the terms plaintiff and defendant.
5. What is the object of primary elections, and who are entitled to vote at them?
6. What is the political status of the children of a resident alien?
7. Who constitutes the electoral college?
8. Define United States consul, and tell in which department of the executive the consular service is embraced.
9. What amendments have been made to the constitution since the Rebellion? Why?

EXAMINATION XVII.

1. Name and define the most common forms of government.
2. Name, and tell in whom the different departments of the federal government are vested.
3. What are the qualifications of a representative?
4. Name the ways in which a bill, having passed both houses, may beome a law.
5. When a vacancy occurs in the representation of a state, how is it filled?
6. When, where, and by whom are the electoral votes counted?
7. What is treason? Letters of marque and reprisal? The writ of habeas corpus?
8. How may a foreigner become a citizen of the United States?
9. What are the qualifications for President? For Vice-President?
10. How may a new state be admitted into the Union?

EXAMINATION XVIII.

1. What branches of government are recognized by the constitution?

2. The relation of the states to the general government, as defined by the constitution.

3. How many members are there in the House of Representatives? By whom are they elected? For what term? How apportioned among the states at first? What made the change? What is a Congressman-at-large?

4. What share has the President in legislation? What is meant by presidential electors? How long does it take to complete the election of a President?

5. What made the last three amendments to the constitution necessary? State the substance of the fourteenth amendment.

EXAMINATION XIX.

1. What conditions of society necessitate government? What should government serve?

2. Why was the present constitution adopted? Give a short history of its adoption.

3. What is the limitation in the constitution of the United States in regard to bills for raising revenue?

4. Define state, alien, citizen and elector.

5. In what two ways may a municipal corporation legally proceed to obtain required funds for any public improvement? Which do you think the better? And why?

6. Discriminate impeachment, indictment.

7. Name the county officers representing the three departments of government.

8. Would the general welfare of the United States be promoted if the national government should be the owner of the railroads and telegraph lines? And why?

EXAMINATION XX.

1. What were the purposes of the constitution of the United States, as set forth in the preamble?

2. Name the three departments of government and describe briefly the functions of each.

CIVIL GOVERNMENT. 103

3. What preliminary steps are required by the constitution in choosing a President of the United States?

4. Name the members of the President's cabinet now in office and mention the state in which each one has his residence.

5. What are the constitutional qualifications concerning eligibility of the President? United States Senators? Members of the House of Representatives? Governor of Pennsylvania? Members of the State Legislature?

EXAMINATION XXI.

1. Presiding officer of Senate, House of Representatives and Supreme Court. How chosen? For what term? What called?

2. What is the writ of habeas corpus? When can it be refused?

3. State five things Congress shall have power to do.

4. State five things Congress cannot do.

EXAMINATION XXII.

1. What were some of the defects in the articles of confederation?

2. Name the qualifications of electors for representatives in Congress.

3. What is an impeachment? By whom made? By whom tried? Who can be impeached? What is the judgment?

4. In what cases are criminals not tried by jury?

5. What is an ex-post facto law?

6. How are vacancies filled in the House of Representatives and Senate?

7. How do the qualifications of a representative differ from those of a Senator?

8. What are letters of marque and reprisal?

9. How does the basis of representation in the House differ from that of the Senate?

10. Can Presidential electors legally vote for whom they please?

EXAMINATION XXIII.

1. Name and define the different forms of government, known in history.

2. Name the departments of our government, and the powers of each.

3. State some advantages of having two houses of Congress.

4. What qualifications must a man have to be eligible to the office of President.

5. If the electors fail to elect a President, and the House of Representatives also fail to elect, who would become President?

6. What are the duties of the President of the United States?

7. What officers constitute his cabinet?

8. How may a bill become a law notwithstanding the President's veto?

9. Give a full explanation of a writ of habeas corpus.

10. In framing the constitution why were the smaller states allowed equal representation with the larger states in the Senate.

10. PHYSIOLOGY AND HYGIENE.

A Mastery of the Parts, With Their Functions, and of the Different Processes Required in this Branch and a Thorough Acquaintance With Laws of Health and Especially With Their Application.

PHYSIOLOGY AND HYGIENE.

EXAMINATION I.

1. Define anatomy, physiology, hygiene.
2. Describe the capillaries.
3. Discuss narcotics: their uses and abuses.
4. How do we "catch a cold?" How can we cure it?
5. What changes does the air undergo in the lungs? The blood?
6. How does alcohol affect the heart? The brain?
7. Describe the digestion, assimilation and absorption of a piece of bread and butter.
8. Describe the skin. Tell its uses.
9. How can the same eye see different objects at different distances?
10. Give at least two good ways of ventilating a school room.

EXAMINATION II.

1. What is meant by digestion?
2. Give structure of a tooth.
3. Give the number and situation of the teeth. Name each kind.
4. Give usual classification of foods, with examples of each class.
5. Describe the alimentary canal.
6. Describe: (a) the salivary glands, (b) the liver, (c) the pancreas, (d) the spleen.
7. Describe the stomach.
8. Describe the action of: (a) saliva. (b) gastric juice. (c) bile. (d) pancreatic juice. (e) intestinal juice.
9. How is absorption accomplished?
10. Describe the lacteals and lymphatics.

EXAMINATION III.

1. Give the structure, use and composition of bones. Give the divisions of the skeleton.
2. Name and describe the two classes of muscles.
3. Describe the heart and greater circulation.
4. What effect has alcohol on (a) the blood vessels, (b) nerves, (c) muscles?
5. Name the necessary foods, and explain the process of digestion.
6. Describe the eye. How do we see?
7. Give the directions for ventilation and the general care of the body.
8. Give rules for the care of the eyes.

EXAMINATION IV.

1. Give the structure, composition and uses of the bones.
2. Describe the structure and functions of the skin.
3. Name the various processes in the conversion of food into tissue.
4. Name the digestive fluids and the organs that secrete them.
5. Describe the heart, and trace the blood in its course through the body.
6. Describe lymph and the lymphatics.
7. What changes take place in the air during respiration? In the blood?
8. Give the divisions of the brain, the functions of each, and tell how the brain is protected.
9. What is reflex action? Describe the reflex actions of the sympathetic nervous system.
10. Locate, describe, and give the function of the crystalline lens; of the retina; of the iris.

EXAMINATION V.

1. Decribe the spinal column.
2. Define ligament and cartilage, and give the use of each.

3. Name the different fluids of the human body.
4. Give the structure of muscles, and define flexors and extensors.
5. Give the structure and functions of the skin.
6. State the importance of bathing.
7. Describe the stomach, and give the organs that absorb the food.
8. State the effect of alcohol upon digestion.
9. What things should be observed to secure healthy digestion?
10. Define nervous system and give the functions of the gray and white matter.
11. Give the functions of the parts of the brain.
12. Name the special senses.

EXAMINATION VI.

1. Form and composition of bones.
2. Discuss gastric digestion.
3. Discuss absorption.
4. Discuss the uses of the blood.
5. Describe the lungs and the changes in the air from respiration.
6. The coats and humors of the eye, and make diagram.
7. The spinal cord and its functions.
8. Describe the effects of alcohol on the brain, stomach and liver.

EXAMINATION VII.

1. What are the four principal elements of organized bodies?
2. Explain the construction of the joints.
3. Name the divisions and valves of the heart, and give the special use of each of the valves.
4. Name the fluids of digestion and the organ or organs by which each fluid is secreted.
5. What important operations are performed in the

capillaries? What relation do the capillaries bear to the arteries and veins?

6. What difference in the functions of the lymphatics and the lacteals?

7. Name the respiratory organs, and describe the lungs.

8. What distinction in the functions of the cerebrum and the cerebellum?

9. In how many minutes will fifty pupils vitiate the air in an unventilated room twenty-five feet square and twelve feet high?

10. What is the composition of pure air?

EXAMINATION VIII.

1. Define physiology, comparative anatomy, inorganic bodies.

2. Salivary glands and their office.

3. Functions of the nervous system.

4. Hearing apparatus.

EXAMINATION IX.

1. Define physiology.

2. Define the osseous system; tell how many bones are in the human system, and how they are divided.

3. How many teeth are in each set, and name the teeth in the permanent set.

4. Define circulation and describe it from the entrance of the blood into the right auricle.

5. Define digestion, and name all the processes succeeding prehension.

6. Explain the formation of the ear and the functions of the various parts.

7. Explain the structure of the brain, names of various parts, and functions of gray and white matter.

8. Define muscle, and name several uses of muscles.

9. Explain the construction of the organs of voice.

10. Name the five senses, and locate each sensation to its appropriate organ.

EXAMINATION X.

1. The various joints, and the description of the one at the shoulder.
2. The structure, action and arrangement of the mucles.
3. Why is the effect of alcohol felt so soon, when taken?
4. Name an albuminous substance, and its nutritive principle.
5. State the difference between arterial blood and venous blood.
6. Nervous matter and reflex action.
7. What are condiments? Antidotes? Narcotics?
8. Where do you find the pericardium? The periosteum? The diaphram? The tendons?

EXAMINATION XI.

1. Describe the composition, structure and uses of bones.
2. Describe the structure and functions of the skin and its adjuncts.
3. Explain, as far as you are able, the various activities that take place in or in immediate connection with the stomach during digestion.
4. Describe the various provisions which are made for the protection of the brain.
5. Explain and give examples of automatic nervous action.
6. Explain, as clearly as possible for you, the physiological effects that come from inadequate ventilation, and show how you would determine whether the air of a room is in good or bad condition.
7. Draw an outline of the thorax and the organs contained within it, and then give a brief description of the structure and functions of each of these organs.
8. By means of a diagram and its explanation, show the nature of nearsightedness and its remedy.

PHYSIOLOGY AND HYGIENE. 111

9. Locate the liver, describe its immediate surroundings, its structure and uses.

10. Write upon the topics:
1. Effects of alcohol upon the human system.
2. Hygiene of the school room.

EXAMINATION XII.

1. Describe the whole process of breathing, and the air as an article of food.

2. State the principal objects to be secured by ventilation and mention the best methods of admitting air into a room.

3. How does bathing affect the temperature of the body?

4. Describe the various structures and processes through which the food passes into the circulation.

5. Will sugar and albumen injected into the veins assimilate? Explain.

6. What changes are produced in the brain by the use of alcohol?

7. Explain the difference between the sensation of touch and that of pain.

EXAMINATION XIII.

1. Discuss the skin and its uses.
2. What is meant by assimilation.
3. Mention three kinds of food, and give an example of each.
4. Discuss the food nature of alcohol.
5. Describe the effects of alcohol on the heart; on the nervous system.
6. Where should a bleeding artery be compressed to stop the flow of blood? A vein?
7. Describe the ear.
8. Discuss exercise.

9. Name the organs of respiration and give the results accomplished by them.

10. Of what kind of nerve matter are the ganglia mainly composed? What is the office of white nerve matter? What that of gray nerve matter?

EXAMINATION XIV.

1. (a) Describe the human skeleton.
   (b) Distinguish organ from function.
2. (a) Describe the process of digestion.
   (b) Distinguish chyme from chyle.
3. (a) Describe circulation, organs and uses.
   (b) Compare arteries and veins.
4. Describe respiration, organs and uses.
5. (a) Describe the eye.
   (b) Give normal temperature of the body.

EXAMINATION XV.

1. Define the osseous system, and name five bones of the head, five of the trunk, five of the arms and five of the legs.
2. Describe the circulation, beginning with the blood in the right auricle.
3. Describe the nervous system.
4. Describe the various processes of digestion.
5. Define a stimulant, an opiate, a narcotic.
6. What are the effects of alcohol upon the human system?

EXAMINATION XVI.

1. What is the distinction between organic and inorganic matter?
2. What functions are peculiar to animals alone, and what are they called?
3. Compare the heart and lungs giving three points in common, three points of difference.

4. Tell the principal uses of bones, of what composed, how many and how divided.

5. Muscles:
  (a) What are they?
  (b) Of how many kinds?
  (c) Their characteristics and what does each imply?
  (d) Their uses.
  (e) The effect of exercise upon them.

6. Name the digestive organs.

7. What are the heat-producing organs and what is the present readily accepted theory of animal heat.

EXAMINATION XVII.

1. State the composition and use of bones. Name the bones of the head.
2. Name the organs of respiration.
3. Describe digestion and assimilation.
4. Describe the circulation of the blood.
5. Name and describe the different parts of the eyeballs.
6. Name and describe the different parts of the brain.
7. Name the special senses, and the nerves of special sense.

II. VOCAL MUSIC.

This Art Includes Sight Reading, the Proper Managements of the Voice, the Theory of Vocal Music and Methods of Teaching the Subject. The Final Examinations are Generally Oral.

VOCAL MUSIC.

EXAMINATION I.

1. What is a musical sound called?
2. Of what is the clef composed; by what is it divided, and what is the division called?
3. What is a clef? Give lines and spaces of each.
4. What is an interval? Give example.
5. Explain formation of a scale.
6. How are keynotes in sharps and flats found respectively?
7. What interval is changed in flats, what tone raised?
8. Write six measures in 6-8 time, introducing in sharps.
9. Write the scale whose signature is four flats.

EXAMINATION II.

1. Define measure.
2. Write: (a) four double measures, **(b) four triple** measures, (c) four quadruple measures.
3. Define scale.
4. Write two diatonic major scales.
5. Define: (a) signature, (b) how does a sharp effect a tone?
6. Define: (a) diatonic scale, (b) major scale.
7. Define: (a) interval, (b) how are intervals named?
8. Illustrate kinds of intervals.

9. Write thirds in key of G, marking each with its Roman numeral.

10. Write following exercise on staff in key of G:

$\frac{4}{4}$, 3, 2, 1, 0, | 0-2- | 3, 1, | 5-4, 3, | 2-6, 2, | 1, 8, 1-||

NOTE.—The class was drilled on chart work and sight reading in the presence of the Board.

EXAMINATION III.

1. What is the key of this piece? How can you tell? Where is *do* found in the soprano? In the bass? What is time of the piece? What is the first note in the alto?

2. How can you tell whether a note is high or low in the tonic-sol-fa-system?

3. Sing the notes of this piece—now sing the words.

4. What is the difference between the natural key and the key of one sharp? Where do the half-tones naturally occur?

5. In changing the keys in flats, to what number do we go? To what number do we go in changing to sharps?

6. How many lines and spaces are used in music? What is the name of the first line, first space, second space, etc?

7. What is the difference between the treble clef and soprano clef? What do you mean by the G clef? By the F clef?

8. What do the fractions at the begining of a piece of music signify? What the numerator, the denominator?

9. Sing one, two, three, four.

10. Is this a new piece? Read the notes in the soprano. In the bass.

EXAMINATION IV.

1. (a) Define measure. (b) Name the kinds.

2. Write the following exercise on the staff in the key of G.

$\frac{3}{4}$ sol, sol, mi, | fa | mi, | o | la, | si, re, do.||

(comma after a syllabble signifies quarter note. Dash after a syllable signifies half note. Cipher indicates a rest.)

3. (a) Define slur. (b) Define tie.
4. Define scale.
5. Define diatonic scale.
6. (a) Define signature. (b) How does a sharp affect a tone?
7. What two kinds of scales are represented in the scale of C? Why?
8. Define an interval.
9. Name in order, the kinds of intervals in the following exercise. (a) From G.—B. (b) From A.—C. (c) From A.—B. (d) G. (e) From G.—G. (f) From G.—E. (g) From F.—E.
10. Write the thirds in the key of G, marking each with its Roman numeral.

EXAMINATION V.

1. Define and give an example of a flat, a syncopated note, a clef, an accidental, a tie.
2. What is the difference between the diatonic and chromatic scales? Illustrate.
3. Draw a staff and place upon it the G clef, the signature of the key of B, the time mark for some variety of sextuple measure, and fill three measures with notes and rests.
4. What is meant by transposition of the scale? Give the methods of transposition and illustrate each.
5. Give the meaning of the following: Andante, mp., cres., D. S., Rit.

EXAMINATION VI.

1. On what syllable do we get tone one, tone three?
2. How many tones in the scale?
3. How many one-half tones in the scale, and where do they come?

4. What is the difference of pitch between two scales called?
5. How many necessary properties have sounds.
6. Of what do melodies treat?
7. What are musical sounds called?
8. What is essential pitch of tones called?
9. What are used as the absolute pitch of sounds?
10. Why use one sharp as signature of G?
11. What do you mean by change of key?
12. Transposition by one sharp is by what?
13. What is the other transposition called?
14. How many 16ths would you sing in the tone of $\frac{1}{8}$?
15. Repeat, how indicated? What is a bar? A measure? How is time indicated.
16. Discuss the value of a knowledge of vocal music.

(120)

12. BOOK-KEEPING.

Single Entry, Equivalent to a Daily Exercise of at Least Seven Weeks. Examinations are Frequently Oral and Written Combined.

BOOK-KEEPING.

EXAMINATION I.

1. What is book-keeping? Why is it a science? Why an art?

2. How many books would you use in single entry? What is the object of the day-book? Of the ledger?

3. Name some of the essentials of posting from the day-book to the ledger? What things would you post into the ledger?

4. What is the object of the cash-book? How do you make entries in the cash-book? How do you enter a check?

5. Dictate a receipt for part payment of a debt. How does a receipt for part payment differ from one for payment in full?

6. If by mistake a receipt in full is given for part of debt, how can the remainder be collected?

7. What do you mean by available means?

8. Dictate a form of check for ten dollars, payable at First National Bank, Bloomsburg.

9. I owe you $30, payable in six months, and I want to pay you with a check, how much shall I make it? Shall it be written or order or bearer? Would a check written or bearer be paid to any one who had it?

10. You have taught six months and the treasurer pays you, give him a receipt.

11. You have a store, and I come to pay my account, to what book would you turn to find my account.

12. You want to apply for a grammar school, dictate an application.

13. Dictate a letter of introduction for a friend in Philadelphia.

EXAMINATION II.

1. What is book-keeping?
2. Define debtor and creditor.
3. Name five business papers.
4. Write a note in your favor, indorse in full and in blank.
5. Define negotiable papers.
6. What books are used in single entry.
7. Write three debit and three credit entries in which the debit are the greater.
8. Pass those entries and close the account.
9. When should red ink be used.
10. State signature for men or women.

EXAMINATOIN III.

1. Of what use is a receipt. Write one showing you have received your salary for one month as teacher.
2. Define indorsement, and state its use to a business man.
3. State the difference between a draft and check, and their advantage in business.
4. Illustrate with the following items, the use of the day-book, cash-book and ledger.
   (a) June 4. Sold J. A. Angle, on account, pens. Sold Andrew White, slates. Sold Kate Wilson, pen holders. Bought of Porter and Coates, Philadelphia, Pa., ink, pens and chalk. Write the invoice.
   (b) June 5, received of J. A. Angel, amount in full. Sold Andrew White, readers. Sold J. A. Angel, rulers and pens.

(c) June 6, sent Porter and Coates check in payment for goods, per invoice.

(d) Sold drawing books for cash. Sold Kate Wilson copy books.

(e) June. 7, received of Kate Wilson, draft for payment in full. Draft to be drawn on Henry James and indorsed in favor of A. T. Stewart. Received of Andrew White, his note at sixty days, for payment in full.

(f) Cash on hand at opening of cash-book, $40.

5. Why are some of the entries made in the day-book, some in the cash-book and some in both?

EXAMINATION IV.

1. Write a check for $50 payable to my order.

2. Suppose you wish to borrow $300 from a bank for 30 days. Explain how you would do it, and write the promissory note you would use.

3. Describe the books a retail dry goods merchant should keep.

EXAMINATION V.

1. Discuss the importance of a knowledge of business forms.

2. Write an order for your first month's salary on treasurer, signed by secretary and president.

3. Write a receipt in full—a receipt to apply on account.

4. Make out a bill of goods, and receipt it.

5. Write a promissory note with self as the maker. Who first endorses a note?

6. Write a check—Define parties to a check. What do you mean by a certified check?

7. To settle a bill what book do you first turn to? How find the page? What would be shown on the page? Where would you find the items? How find the page in day-book?

8. What books other than those mentioned are sometimes used? Explain the use of each.

9. Is everything first written in the day-book?

10. How would you use an order? Should it be endorsed to get the money? Can a stranger get an order cashed?

11. Can you get a check cashed at a bank in which you have no deposit?

12. Who protests a note, and under what circumstances?

13. If you should send an unendorsed check in which you are the payee to Philadelphia, what would be done with it?

14. Explain difference between check and draft.

15. When would you endorse a check received from another person, to obtain the money?

16. How draw money from a bank for your own use?

EXAMINATION VI.

1. How would you open your books on commencing business?

2. How would you open the cash account? State how to post cash received and paid.

3. How would you find at end of year your gain or loss.

4. Write a promissory note for $200, dating from to-day to October 1, 1885.

13. DRAWING.

A Daily Exercise of at Least Twenty-Eight Weeks. **Work** to be Submitted to the Examining Board.

DRAWING.

EXAMINATION I.

1. What is drawing?
2. Of what use is drawing to the teacher?
3. Name and define straight lines used in drawing.
4. Name and define curved lines used in drawing.
5. Illustrate straight and curved lines by combining in a figure.
6. Give rule for drawing vertical, horizontal and slanting lines.
7. In what order should the lines be drawn?
8. Where is generally the best place to begin a drawing?
9. Define and illustrate right, acute and oblique angles.
10. What is the difference between straight and curved lines?

EXAMINATION II.

1. An object drawing leson, examination of test sheets, and black board work.
2. What is drawing?
3. What is perspective drawing, and name kind of objects.
4. In perspective drawing how would parallel lines seem to be.
5. How far off can you represent an object in perspective drawing?
6. What is utility of shade?
7. How would you represent the image of the earth upon the moon?

8. Name advantages arising from knowledge of perspective drawing.

9. How do we represent distance in a drawing?

10. How do we get an idea of form.

11. Which is more beautiful, a straight or curved line? Why?

EXAMINATION III.

1. Name, define and draw the different triangles.

2. What is an elipse? Draw one.

3. How do lines vanish when an object is situated either above or below the eye line?

4. How much time would you devote to drawing in an ungraded school?

5. Construct a hexagon, side, two inches.

6. Draw a simple design in an equilateral triangle, suitable for dictation to a class of young children.

7. Inscribe a pentagon in a circle, diameter four inches.

(130)

14. ARITHMETIC.

Complete. A Very Thorough Course is Required in Both Written and Mental. In Some Schools the Mental is Taught Separately; but the Examinations Combine the Two.

ARITHMETIC.

EXAMINATION I.

NOTE—Give outlines of the work. Do not write out the questions, use the numbers.

1. Reduce $\frac{3\frac{1}{3}}{.025}$ to a decimal fraction and subtract from it $\frac{3}{4}$ of .01.

2. The longitude of Boston is 71° 4′ W., what is the time (and the day) by the sun at Boston when it is 3.35 A. M., June 2, in London (longitude 0° 5′ W.)?

3. In 1886 the wages of mechanics in Massachusetts were 25 per cent. higher, while the prices of things were 20 per cent. lower than in 1860. If in 1886 a mechanic received $90 per month, how much money could he have saved during the year, supposing that he saved nothing in 1860, and that he had kept the same standard of living with no additional expenses, as in 1860.

4. Write a 60-day note, dated to-day, and payable at some Pennsylvania bank. If discounted on July 12, find proceeds.

5. How much higher is a gallon measure than a quart measure of similar shape? Answer to be correct to nearest hundredth.

EXAMINATION II.

1. The holder of a 75-day note received $559 as proceeds when the note was discounted at 4 per cent. What was the face of the note?

A gentleman left $\frac{1}{3}$ of his property to his elder son, $\frac{1}{5}$ to his younger son, $\frac{1}{6}$ to his daughter, and the balance,

ARITHMETIC. 133

$369.75, to a charitable institution. How much did each receive?

3. Extract the square root of 2672.5879, and divide this root by twenty-five ten thousandths.

4. A person bought a certain number of barrels of flour for $4,400. He reserved 40 barrels for his own use and sold ⅞ of the remainder for $3,952, which was $608 more than cost, find the number of barrels he bought.

5. How many quarts of berries at 27 cents a quart will pay for 14⅖ yards of carpet at $1.87½ a yard?

EXAMINATION III.

1. 5 gals., 2 qts., 1 pt. of jelly were put in half-pint jars which cost 5 cts. each; the jelly was sold at 12½ cts. per jar. What was left after paying for the jars?

2. A man owing a debt paid ⅔ of it, and afterwards paid ¾ of the remainder. To make the second payment required $195.60 less than to make the first. Find the debt.

3. How much more than $3 per day must a man receive in order that he pay a bill of 42\frac{9}{10}$, or of $70⅕, or of $97½, and use in each case the entire pay for a whole number of days?

4. Sand weighs three times as much as water. A tub full of water weighs 150lbs, and full of sand 400lbs. Find weight of tub and how many gallons it holds.

5. When it is noon at Greenwich what is the time at this school.

6. A invests $7,200, in 5 per cent. stock bought at 90, while B invests the same amount in 8 per cent. stock bought at 144. What is the difference in their annual income?

EXAMINATION IV.

1. Define: Concrete number, abstract number, multiple, denominate number, ratio and proportion.

2. How many figures are required to express 125 octillion by the English method?

3. Write the prime numbers between 40 and 60. Find the G. C. D. of 115 and 161.

4. Which is heavier and how much an ounce of gold or an ounce of feathers?

5. How many minims in 5 gals. 3 pts. 12 fluid drams, 5 fluid ozs.

6. Reduce 5.6 oz., .825 of a pound and 2 ℔s, 8 cwts., (Troy) to grains.

7. How much must I pay for 10⅔ bus. of rice at the rate of $15¾ for 5¾ bus. Write full analysis.

8. A miller sent his agent $9,270 to be invested in flour at $5 a barrel. How many barrels will be received, the agent being paid 3 per cent. for purchasing.

9. How much must I pay for stock that pays 6 per cent. dividends that I may realize 8 per cent. on my investment?

10. A bought a house for $4,000 and agreed to pay what is due yearly. What will be the sum due at the end of 8 years, interest at 6 per cent.

EXAMINATION V.

1. Define a fraction, and give different kinds. Distinguish between simple, compound and complex, between common and decimal, and proper and improper fractions.

2. A quarter-section of land costs $1,800. What is the cost at the same rate of a field 40 chains long, and 16 chains, 24 links wide.

3. A 5-cent loaf of bread weighs 10 oz., when flour is $6 a barrel, what should it weigh when flour is $7 a barrel?

4. What is the largest size measure which can be filled an exact number of times from any one of three bins, the 1st, holding 38 bus. 1 pk., the 2d, 30 bus., the 3rd, 46 bus. and 2 pks?

5. When it is 10 minutes past 2 P. M., in 56 degrees

east longitude, what time is it in 56 degrees west longitude?

6. A gold eagle weighs 258 grains and the gold coinage of United States is $\frac{1}{10}$ alloy. How many cwt. of pure gold in $100 gold coin?

7. An apothecary buys 10 gallons of spirits at $1.75 a gallon, and sells it at 3 cents a fluid oz. What is his profit?

8. Find the sum of an arithmetic series in which 1st term $= 18$, com. diff. $= 7$, no. term $= 9$.

EXAMINATION VI.

1—(a) Simplify $\dfrac{2+\dfrac{1}{3}}{5+\dfrac{1}{4}}$ (b) $\dfrac{(.38x.00027)+(.057x.0036)}{1-.9487}$

2. What is a prime number? Give example.

3. Which is the faster, a train which runs 225 rods a minute or one which runs a mile in 80 seconds?

4. When it is 7h. 36m. A. M., at Washington, longitude 77° 3′ 37″ W., what time is it at Calcutta, longitude 88° 19′ 2″ E?

5. Define discount, present worth, proportion.

6. An agent sold a consignment of cotton for $10,300, and invested the proceeds in flour at $5 per barrel. If the commission was 3 per cent. for buying and 2 per cent. for selling, how many barrels of flour did he puchase?

7. Find the amount of $26.25 from Dec. 20, 1886, to June 2, 1890, at 6 per cent.

8. A note for $1,500 was dated June 15, 1875, and was due in one year at 6 per cent. It was discounted at a bank February 19, 1876, at 7 per cent. Find day of maturity, term of discount and proceeds.

EXAMINATION VII.

1. What is the advantage of the metric system of weights and measures? Illustrate the system briefly.
2. Explain and illustrate stocks.
3. Explain partnership with time.
4. Explain compound proportion.
5. Explain division of decimals.
6. Explain partial payments.
7. Bought 75 yards of cloth at 10 per cent. less than first cost, and sold them at 10 per cent. more than first cost; gained $25. What was the first cost per yard?
8. What will be the face of a 30-day draft purchased for $1,500, if the rate of exchange be $\frac{1}{8}$ per cent. premium, and the rate of discount be 6 per cent.
9. A and B alone can do a piece of work in 15 and 18 days respectively. They work together for three days, when B leaves; but A continues, and after three days is joined by C. They finish the remainder in four days. In what time could C do the whole work?

EXAMINATION VIII.

1. Simplify $\dfrac{1\frac{1}{4} \times \frac{2}{3}}{5\frac{1}{2}} \div \dfrac{3-\frac{2}{3}}{\frac{1}{2} \text{ of } 7}$.

2. The difference in time between Buffalo and Cleveland being 11 minutes, what is the difference in longitude?
3. What is the exact interest on $140.40 from August 29, 1864, to November 29, 1865, at $6\frac{1}{2}$ per cent.?
4. If a staff 5 ft. casts a shadow 3 ft. how high is a steeple whose shadow at the same time is 90 ft.?
5. A man walks 100 miles in two days, and $\frac{1}{3}$ of the distance walked the first, added to $\frac{1}{4}$ the distance walked the second day, equals half the distance walked the first day; how far did he walk each day?
6. If I buy salt at $\frac{3}{4}$ of a cent a pound, and sell it in butter at 25 cents a pound, what is my gain per cent.

7. If a man gave $18,810 for horses and sold a certain number of them for $7,990, at $85 each, and by so doing lost $10 each; for how much must he sell the remainder to gain $2,180 in the transaction?

8. A triangular box is 6 ft. on a side, and 4 ft. high. How many bushels of wheat will it hold?

9. What would be the cost of 3 sticks of timber 8x10 inches, and 32 ft. long at $12 per thousand feet?

10. The joint stock of a company was $5,400, which was doubled at the end of the year. A put in half for ¾ of a year; B ⅔ for half a year, and C the remainder for one year. How much is each one's share of the entire stock at the end of the year?

EXAMINATION IX.

1. Define composite number, concrete number, least common multiple, cancellation.

2. Find G. C. D. of 392, 448 and 504 by two methods.

3. In what particulars do compound numbers differ from simple, and in what are they alike?

4. Explain how you would find the interest on a sum of money for 3 years, 5 months, and 5 days, at any rate per cent. by two methods.

5. If I buy goods at 16c., how must I mark them in order that I may fall 11½ per cent. from marked price, and still gain 25 per cent?

6. I send my agent $5,000 to invest in coffee, commission 2½ per cent. Coffee having advanced 5 per cent. I intrust him to sell and invest proceeds in Philadelphia 6's at 103¾, brokerage ¼ per cent. How many shares and what surplus?

7. Develop rule for sum of series in arithmetical progression.

Write the analysis of the following:

8. When eggs are worth 40 cts. per doz., how many will it take to buy 8 bus. potatoes worth 62½ cts. per bus.?

9. One-half the difference between two numbers is 6, and ⅛ of the first number equals ¼ of the second; required the numbers.

10. If a man can dig 15 bus. potatoes a day, and can pick up 10 bus. a day, how many can he dig and pick up in one day?

EXAMINATION X.

1. Extract the cube root of .2 to three decimals.
2. Give the units of the metric system.
3. Find the altitude of a triangle if each side is 1,000 feet.
4. When it is noon at Greenwich, the time at Harrisburg is 6 hrs. 52 min. 40 sec. A. M., what is the longitude of Harrisburg?
5. A pipe can fill a cistern in ¼ of an hour and a waste pipe can empty ¼ of it in 20 minutes. If both pipes are opened, in what time can the cistern be filled?
6. What alteration will be made in an income by selling $10,000 four per cent. stocks at 89¼ including brokerage, and buying five per cent. stock at 105 including brokerage?
7. Prove the rule for reducing ⅛ to a decimal fraction.
8. Show that .3 (a repetend) $= \frac{1}{3}$ by the formula for an infinite series, as well as by analysis and by deduction.
9. Write three fractions or fractional expressions that are equal respectively to a finite decimal, to a circulate, and to an infinite decimal not a circulate.

EXAMINATION XI.

1. Reduce $\dfrac{49\frac{7}{10}}{33\frac{1}{3}} \div \dfrac{57\frac{1}{11}}{16\frac{2}{3}}$.
2. Find G. C. D. of $\frac{3}{11}$, $\frac{7}{20}$, $\frac{14}{15}$.
3. $(.005 \div .0025 + \frac{1}{8} - \frac{1}{2}) \times .02\frac{1}{4} \div 1\frac{1}{10} = ?$
4. $\sqrt[3]{34\frac{2}{4}}$.
5. I buy a house January 3, for $4,000, to be paid for in 6 mos. If I pay $1,000 March 3, and $1,000 May 3; when ought I to pay the balance?

ARITHMETIC. 139

6. A and B can do a piece of work in 12 days. How long will it take each to do it, provided A can do only $\frac{2}{3}$ as much as B?

EXAMINATION XII.

1. Find the diameter of a circle of which the number of inches in its circumference is equal to the number of square feet of its area.

2. The diameter of a circle is four feet; find the area of the inscribed equilateral triangle.

3. Find the amount of timber in a log 40 feet long, whose radii are respectively 6 feet and 3 feet.

4. State the formula for finding the surface and volume of a sphere.

5. Construct a problem to find the volume of an irregular body and state the formula of calculating it.

6. Discuss quadrilaterals.

EXAMINATION XIII.

1. The value of a certain fraction whose denominator is 243 is $7\frac{2}{3}$. Find the numerator of the fraction.

2. What per cent. of 6945 must be added to that number to make the sum 7695?

3. What sum of ready money will cancel an indebtedness of $625 due in 4 months 20 days hence, money at 6 per cent. per annum?

4. A cotton broker sold for a planter cotton amounting to $3,860, and gave the purchaser 5 per cent. discount for cash. If the broker retained 2½ per cent. commission on his cash receipts, and paid freight and storage amounting to $51.26, how much should he have remitted to the planter?

5. What is the ratio of seven pounds troy weight to ten ounces avoirdupois.

6. Divide 25 by six hundred twenty-five ten thousandths.

7. From a quartz rock yielding silver at the rate of $123.75 per ton, a miner obtained $103.95 worth; what was the weight of the rock?

8. Find the square root of .065536, and divide the result by one hundred twenty-eight hundred-thousandths.

9. Vienna is 16° 23' east longitude; what is the time there at 9 A. M. New York (longitude 74° 3' west)?

10. Miss Lyle owns 28 shares, at $50, in the Nonesuch Ins. Co., which on account of losses requires an assessment of $3\frac{1}{2}$ per cent.; what does she pay?

EXAMINATION XIV.

I.

Submit answers only to the following examples:

1. Change twenty-three-fortieths to a decimal fraction.
2. Change .1250 to a common fraction.
3. Divide .0003 by 3.75.
4. Find the exact interest of $1,560 for 93 days at 6 per cent.
5. Find the cube root of 633839.779.

II.

Submit work in full of the following problems:

6. I bought Pennsylvania railroad stock at $48.50 a share. The dividends are 5 per cent. on the par value, which is $50. What interest do I get on my investment?

7. I bought a lot at $5 a linear foot, street front. The depth of the lot is 360 feet. What did the land cost me an acre?

8. If you start at St. Louis, latitude 38°, 37', 28" North, and travel north 1,800 miles, what latitude will you reach?

9. The hypotenuse of a right triangle is 115 feet and the base 92 feet; what is the perpendicular?

10. A stand pipe is 80 feet high, and 10 feet in diameter. How many gallons of water does it contain?

III.

Why are the "terms" of a fraction named as they are? What do you mean by the "principles of fractions?"

IV.

What method of subtraction do you prefer? Why? What is the relation between multiplication and addition?

V.

Of what use is the study of arithmetic? To what extent should it be studied?

EXAMINATION XV.

1. Define and illustrate a denominate number, bank discount, par value, the cube root of a number.
2. $\frac{2}{3}$ of A's money equals $32, and $\frac{2}{3}$ B's money equals $\frac{3}{4}$ of A's; how much has each? (Write solution.)
3. Mr. Allen bought $1,236 worth of dry goods on 8 months time, at 6 per cent.; at the end of two months he borrowed money at 4 per cent. and paid for the goods; what did he gain?
4. A can do as much work in 3 hours as B can do in 5 hours. How long will it take A to finish a piece of work of which B has done $\frac{3}{4}$ in 20 days?? (Write solution.)
5. The proceeds of a note of $350, which had 3 months to run, discounted at a bank at 6 per cent. were invested in wool at 35 cents a pound. How many pounds were bought?
6. Find the length of the diagonal of a square field whose sides are the square root of 2,025.
7. My agent sold my house and lot for $4,850, and then bought me a new house and lot for $3,725; if his commission for selling was 4 per cent. and for buying 2 per cent. how much cash should I receive?

142　　　FINAL EXAMINATION QUESTIONS.

8. Explain and illustrate:
 1. Multiplication of fractions.
 2. Division of decimals.
 3. Three cases of percentage.
 4. Compound proportion.

EXAMINATION XVI.

1. Write out such an explanation as you would give your pupils for inverting the terms of the divisor in division of fractions.

2. A merchant bought a cargo of flour for $2,173$\frac{1}{2}$, and sold it for $\frac{2}{3}$ of the cost, thereby losing $\frac{3}{4}$ of a dollar per barrel; how many barrels did he buy?

3. A drover bought horses for $19,550; he sold a certain number for $8,925, at $105 each, by which he lost $10 a piece; how must he sell the remaining horses, each, to gain $425 on the drove?

4. A merchant selling groceries gives $14\frac{9}{16}$ oz. for a pound; how much does he cheat a customer who buys from him to the amount of $38.40.

5. Develop rule for finding last term, and also the rule for finding sum of series in arithmetical progression.

6. A man borrowed $7,500 and at the end of 2 years, 9 months and 18 days he paid $9,180 to secure his note; what rate of interest did he pay?

7. The end of a minute hand of a clock passes over 31,-416 inches in 40 minutes; what is the length of the hand?

8. Explain fully why you double the quotient for a new divisor in extracting the square root of a number. In extracting cube root of a number why do you point off into periods of 3 places each, and what is the meaning of the numbers 30 and 300 which appear?

9. A receives a 6 per cent dividend on his mining stock and invests it in stock of the same company at 75; the par value of his stock was then $10,800; what was the amount of his dividend?

ARITHMETIC. 143

10. The sales of a certain merchant amount to $100,000 a year, ¼ of the sales are made at a profit of 25 per cent. $\frac{9}{20}$ at a profit of 20 per cent. and the remainder at a loss of 4 per cent.; required the cost of the goods. (Write a complete solution of one of the problems in this list.)

EXAMINATION XVII.

1. Explain the difference between true discount and bank discount and simple interest and bank discount.

2. Extract the cube root of 15625 either by analytic or synthetic solution, and from it derive rule.

3. Find the face of a 90 day note discounted at a bank in New York on the 10th day after its date, the net proceeds being $1,870 and the rate 7 per cent.

4. A reservoir for water is 100 feet long, 64 feet wide and 10 feet deep. The bottom and sides are lined with plank which cost 2½ cents per square foot. Had the reservoir been a cube of equal capacity how much would have been saved in the cost of the plank for lining it?

5. A grocer bought a quantity of flour for $2,400 and having kept it 3 months he sold it at an advance of 20% on 9 months credit. What did he gain, money being worth 6 per cent.

6. A merchant paid 2 cents for the first yard of cloth, 5 cents for the second, 8 cents for the third, etc.; how much did he pay for 75 yards?

7. I wish a vessel of tin, the diameter of the bottom of which is 7 inches, the diameter to diminish 1 inch in rising 3 inches, that shall hold 1 gallon wine measure. How high must it be made?

8. Henry bought a number of pigs for $48, and losing 3 of them he sold ⅔ of the remaining minus 2 for cost, receiving $32 less than all cost. Require the number purchased.

9. A and B agree to mow a field of grass for $60: A mows twice as much as B, lacking 8 acres, and receives $24. How many acres does each mow?

EXAMINATION XVIII.

1. Define number, mathematics, problem, G. C. D., ratio, reciprocal, evolution, discount, annuity, brokerage.

2. If $12\frac{2}{5}$ bus. of corn buy $7\frac{2}{5}$ yds. of cloth, how many bushel will buy $19\frac{1}{2}$ yds?

3. First term is 100, last term 4, common dif. 4; find numbers of terms.

4. What will it cost to cover with gold leaf worth 9 cts. per sq. yd., a cube whose contents are 405,224 cu. yds.?

5. Write the principles of G. C. measure, of percentage.

6. Show why in division of fractions we invert the divisor and multiply? Why $\frac{1}{3}$ cannot be reduced to a pure decimal.

7. A merchant marked his goods at an advance of 60 per cent. and gave a customer 15 per cent. off the marked price. What was his gain on $6.80 received from that customer?

EXAMINATION XIX.

1. What part of $\frac{4}{5}$ is $\frac{2}{3}$?

2. .0003 divided by 3.75.

3. A's age is $1\frac{3}{4}$ times B's and $\frac{2}{3}$ of A's age 2 years ago = $\frac{1}{5}$ of B's age 2 years hence, what is the age of each?

4. A's gain at wholesale is $12\frac{1}{2}$ per cent. and his retail price is 5 per cent. more than his wholesale, what is his gain per cent. at retail?

5. What must I pay for Philadelphia 6's to gain 7 per cent. on the investment?

6. What time of day is it when $\frac{1}{2}$ the time past noon = $\frac{1}{5}$ of the time past midnight?

7. A 60-day note for $350 without interest was paid in 90 days, what was the amount due?

8. If stock bought at 10 per cent. above par, pay 8 per cent. on the investment, what per cent. will it pay if bought at 10 per cent discount?

ARITHMETIC. 145

9. What is the depth of a cubical cistern that contains 1600 gals. of water, each gal. 231 cubic inches.

10. It is between 1 and 2 o'clock and the minute hand is as far past 2 as the hour hand is before it, what is the time.

EXAMINATION XX.

1. Give and demonstrate the rule for dividing one common fraction by another.

2. Divide $5.9001 \frac{3}{7}$ by $.174 \frac{1.125}{18\frac{3}{4}}$ (to 3 decimal places and common fraction.)

3. A room is 33 ft. long and 16 ft. 4 in. wide. How many yards of brussels carpet, $\frac{3}{4}$ yd. wide, will cover it, allowing nothing for waste (answer in yards and common fractions of a yard).

4. A certain field is 40 rods long and 32 rods wide; what are the dimensions of a similar field containing $4\frac{1}{2}$ acres?

5. Which holds the greater number of barrels ($31\frac{1}{6}$ gallons) of water, a cistern 5 feet in diameter and 8 feet deep, or one 6 feet in diameter and 6 feet deep, and how much more (barrels and decimals of a barrel to 2 decimal places)?

6. Draw, dated to-day, a note for one month, payable at the Bloomsburg National Bank, whose proceeds shall be $300 (discount, legal rate in Pennsylvania).

7. The stock of the First National Bank of Bloomsburg, sells at 300, par 100, and yields a dividend of 12 per cent. per annum; the stock of the National Bank of Chester county, sells at $66 (par $25.) and pays 12 per cent.; which pays the better interest on the investment, and how much?

10

15. ALGEBRA.

To Quadratic Equations.   Completed in Senior Year.

ALGEBRA.

EXAMINATION I.

Please copy each question before answering it. Do not give results merely, but indicate your method of solution.

1. Define and give examples of (a) homogeneous quantity; (b) binomial factors; (c) exponent; (d) negative quantity; (e) infinite series.

2. (a) Find the highest common factor of $1-2x+x^2$, $1-x^2$, and $2(y-xy)$. (b) What factors of these quantities would you use to find their lowest common multiple?

3. (a) Find the value of x in $19-(3+x)=20+5(3x-4)$. (b) Give a reason for each step in the work.

4. Find two numbers, the sum of which is 70, such that the second divided by the first gives 2 as a quotient and 1 as a remainder.

5. $5-x\left\{\dfrac{7}{2}-\dfrac{2}{x}\right\}=\dfrac{x}{2}-\dfrac{3x-(4-5x)}{4}$. Find value of x.

6. Write the second number of the following equations:
   (a) $(5x^2-2y^3)^4=$
   (b) $\dfrac{\sqrt[4]{81}}{\sqrt[3]{54ac^7}}=$

7. $\sqrt{x^2-x}=x-\tfrac{1}{2}\sqrt{x}$. Find the value of x.

8. (a) Find the sum of 5 terms of the series 1, .2, .04, etc. (b) Develop the formulas or rules used in your solution.

9. The sum of the squares of two consecutive numbers is 113. What are the numbers?

10. Find two numbers such that their sum multiplied by the greater equals 77 and their difference multiplied by the less number equals 12.

EXAMINATION II.

(Give outlines of the work. Do not write out the questions, use the numbers.)

1. Simplify $14 - \{-7+3(-\overline{4+x})-x\} - \{-[-(-\overline{x-4})]\}$

2. Resolve into prime factors $x^{2m}-y^{2m}$, a^6-a^3, $a^4-c^3+4b^4 +4a^2b^2$, $1+a^6$.

3. What is the value of m o? Prove.

4. Find the value of x in $\dfrac{x-ax}{\sqrt{x}} = \dfrac{x^{\frac{1}{4}}}{x^{-\frac{1}{1}}}$

5. The sum of two numbers is three times the reciprocal of $\frac{1}{3}$, and the sum of their cubes is 189. Find the numbers.

EXAMINATION III.

1. Divide $12a^{5n-3} - a^{4n-2} - 20a^{3n-1} \times 19a^{2n} - 10a^{n+1}$ by $4a^{2n} - 3a^{n+1} + 2a^2$

2. Resolve into factors (a) $1 - 20b + 100b^2$
   (b) $4a^2c - 9c^3$
   (c) $a^2 - b^2 + 2bc - c^2$

3. Find value of x in $\dfrac{x+a}{b} - x = b - \dfrac{x-b}{c} + \dfrac{c-bx}{b}$

4. If the length of a rectangle were 4 feet less, and the width three feet more the figure would be a square of the same area as the given rectangle. Find the dimensions of the rectangle.

5. Find value of x, y and z in $\frac{1}{x} - \frac{2}{y} + 4 = 0$

$\frac{1}{y} - \frac{1}{z} + 1 = 0$

$\frac{2}{z} + \frac{3}{x} - 14 = 0$

6. Write a radical expression, a surd, an imaginary quantity.

7. Define power, coefficient, term, binomial.

8. A can do a piece of work in a days; B, in b days, and C, the same piece in c days. In how many days will they finish it when all work together?

EXAMINATION IV.

1. Define coefficient, exponent, polynomial term, symbols of aggregation, quadratic.

2. Give rule for use of signs in multplication and division.

3. $\{(a-2b+ab)-(a-b+c)\} - \{a-(a-b+ab)\} = ?$

4. $(a^6 - b^6) \div (a^3 - 2a^2b + 2ab^2 - b^3)$.

5. $(x-5)(x-2)-(x-5)(2x-5)+(x+7)(x-2) = 2$.

6. Given $y + \frac{x}{2} = 41$. $x + z = 20\frac{1}{2}$. $y + \frac{3}{5} = 34$ to find x, y, z.

7. Multiply $5x^{-4} + 7x^{-3} + 44x^{-2} + 7x^{-1} + 1$ by $5x^{-2} - 7x^{-1} + 1$.

8. $\sqrt{x} + \sqrt{x-7} = \frac{21}{\sqrt{x-7}}$ to find x.

9. A square fish pond has a walk around it. The side of the pond lacks 2 rods of being six times the width of the walk, and the number of square rods in the walk exceeds the number of rods in the perimeter of the pond by 164, require the area of the pond.

10. Two cubical blocks of marble whose united lengths are 20 inches, contain 2,240 cubic inches, require the surface of each.

EXAMINATION V.

1. Simplify: $\dfrac{x-1+\dfrac{6}{x-6}}{x-2+\dfrac{3}{x-6}}$

2. Find G. C. D. of:
$x^6+x^5-11x+9$ and x^6-6x+5.

3. A and B can earn \$49 in 10 days; A and C can earn \$51 in 10 days; and B and C can earn \$22 in 4 days. How many dollars can each earn in one day.

4. The difference between the total surfaces of two cubes is 144 square inches, and the sum of the edges of the first minus the sum of the edges of the second is 24 inches. Find the length of the edge of each cube.

5. Solve: $\begin{cases} x-3=y+z \\ x+y+z=5 \\ x+y=z-7 \end{cases}$

6. Solve: $\begin{cases} \dfrac{1}{x^2}-\dfrac{1}{y^2}=21 \\ \dfrac{1}{x}-\dfrac{1}{y}=3 \end{cases}$

EXAMINATION VI.

1. $\left\{\dfrac{a}{x+a}-\dfrac{x}{x-a}\right\} \times \left\{\dfrac{x}{a}-\dfrac{a}{x}\right\}$

2. Find the square root of
$$49x^4-28x^3-17x^2+6x+\dfrac{9}{4}$$

3. Simplify:
$3x\sqrt{\dfrac{3a}{4b^2}}+2x\sqrt{\dfrac{a}{3b^2}}-\sqrt{\dfrac{a}{27b^2}}.$

4. There is a number expressed by two digits such that the sum of the squares of the digits is equal to the number increased by the product of the digits, and if 36 is added to the number, the digits will be reversed. What is the number?

5. Solve:
$$\frac{1}{x} + \frac{1}{y} = 3$$
$$\frac{1}{x^2} + \frac{1}{y^2} = 2$$

6. Resolve $4-4x+x^2$ into two factors; then raise one of these factors to the 5th power by the binomial theorem.

EXAMINATION VII.

1. Define algebra, a term, similar terms, an equation.
2. Write a homogeneous trinomial of the 5th degree.
3. Factor: $x^{12}+y^{12}=$
$2a^2x^2+2ax-112=$
4. Solve: $\dfrac{9x+20}{26} = \dfrac{4(x-3)}{5x-4} + \dfrac{x}{4}$

5. A bill of $2.20 is paid in 10 cent pieces and 25 cent pieces. There are 13 coins in all, how many of each?

6. Solve by comparison: $3x-4y=2$.
$7x-9y=7$.

7. Solve: $x^3+y^3=351$.
$x+y=9$.

8. Solve: $(x^2+10)^{\frac{1}{2}}=7x(x^2+10)^{-\frac{1}{2}}$.

9. Find area of a square whose area is increased 175 square inches, by increasing its side 5 inches.

10. Twelve horses and fourteen cows cost $1,900. Five horses and three cows cost $650. Find cost of a horse and of a cow.

ALGEBRA. 153

EXAMINATION VIII.

1. Resolve the following into prime factors:—$(a^{2n}-b^{2n})$; (a^4-1); (a^6-12a^3-13); (x^4-2x^2-24).

2. Given $b - \dfrac{1+x}{1-x} = 0$ to find x.

3. Given $\dfrac{\sqrt{y}}{y} = \dfrac{y-ay}{\sqrt{y}}$ to find y.

4. Given $\sqrt{4x+1} - \sqrt{3} = \sqrt{12}$, to find x.

5. From $3y\sqrt{x} + \dfrac{2x^2}{y-1} - 4x\sqrt{y}$ take $\sqrt{xy^2} + 4x^2 y$.

6. $\begin{Bmatrix} x^2 + 4xy + 4y^2 = 36 \\ x - 2y = 2 \end{Bmatrix}$ to find x and y.

7. Find four geometrical means between 2 and 486.

8. Sold a watch for $171, and the per cent. gained was equal to the number of dollars the watch cost. What was the cost?

9. A square tract of land contains $\frac{1}{4}$ as many acres as are rods in the fence enclosing it. What is the length of the fence?

10. Develop $(a^{\frac{1}{3}} - b^{\frac{1}{3}})^6$ by the binomial theorem.

11. Extract the square root of the following: $a^4 - 2a^3x - a^2x^2 + 2ax^3 + x^4$.

12. $\sqrt{x+5+\sqrt{x+1}} = \sqrt{x+8}$, to find x.

13. Square $21-12\sqrt{3}$.

EXAMINATION IX.

1. Find the greatest common divisor of $5x^2 - 2x - 3$, and $5x^2 - 11x + 6$.

2. Factor $1 + c^3$, also $y^3 - 1$.

3. Expand $(3x-5)^3$.

4. Given $\dfrac{3x-1}{\sqrt{3x}+1} = 1 + \dfrac{\sqrt{3-x}\,1}{2}$ to find the value of x.

5. Given $\begin{Bmatrix} x+y = 10 \\ x\sqrt{y} = 12 \end{Bmatrix}$ to find the value of x and y.

6. A and B together shoot 100 arrows at a target. A put in 11 arrows out of 12, and B 5 arrows out of 8. How many must each shoot that they may put in 80 arrows between them?

7. A person walking along the road in a fog, meets one wagon and overtakes another which is traveling at the same rate as the former, and he observes that between the time of his first seeing and passing the wagons he walks 20 yards and 60 yards respectively. How far can he see in the fog?

8. The continued product of three numbers in geometrical progression is 216, and the sum of the squares of the extremes is 328. What are the numbers?

EXAMINATION X.

1. Give the symbols of operation, and tell what each shows.

2. Multiply $a^{-2} - x^a$ by $a^2 - x^{-a}$. Reduce the result to its simplest form and explain.

3. Factor $x^{2a} - 4x^a - 45$. Tell when and how a trinomial may be factored.

4. Given $\dfrac{x+3}{2} \dfrac{x-2}{3} = \dfrac{3x-5}{12} + \frac{1}{4}$ to find x. Solve and give the reason for each step.

5. Given $\dfrac{x+1}{y-1} - \dfrac{x-1}{y} = \dfrac{6}{y}$ and $x - y = 1$ to find x and y. Name the three methods of elimination, and tell which you use in your work.

6. Given $(x^2 - 4x + 5)^2 + 4x^2 - 16x = -8$ to find x.

7. A square tract of land contained one fourth as many acres as there were rods in the fence surrounding it; required the length of the fence. State, and explain statement.

EXAMINATION XI.

1. Expand $(x - y)^9$ by the binomial theorem.
2. Give first and last three terms of $(x - y)^{100}$.
3. Find the value of $x^{-3} \times x^5$; $x^{-3} \div x^5$; x^{2m} raised to the mth power; mth root of x with an exponent of $5m^4$.
4. Find the root of the equation $x - 2\sqrt{x} = 3$.
5. Find the value of x in $\dfrac{x}{5-x} - \dfrac{5-x}{x} = \dfrac{15}{4}$
6. Find value of the square root of one-half multiplied by the cube root of one-third.
7. Find a number of three places, of which the digits have equal differences in their order. If the number be divided by half the sum of the digits, the quotient will be 41. If 396 be added to the number, the digits will be reversed.

EXAMINATION XII.

1. (a). $a^n - b^n \div a - b$, show that the division terminates.
   (b). Derive the formula for S in both progressions, having given a, n, l.
2. Factor : $3a^3b - 3a^2b - 60ab$.
3. Find x in $2x^2 - 2x + 6\sqrt{2x^2 - 3x + 2} = x + 14$.
4. Reduce $\sqrt[n]{a^{\frac{n}{2}}}$ to a radical of the second degree.
5. Expand $(a-b)^n$ by Bin. Theorem, writing the first three and last two terms.
6. Given $\begin{cases} x^2 + y^2 - x - y = 32 \\ x + y + xy = 29 \end{cases}$, or $\begin{matrix} x^2 - y^2 = 5 \\ x^3y + xy^3 = 78 \end{matrix}$
Find value of x and y.
7. The sum and difference of two numbers is given, to derive a general rule for finding the numbers.
8. The cube root of a certain number is twice its square root; what is the number.

9. The fore wheel of a carriage makes 6 revolutions more than the hind wheel in going a distance of 120 yards. If the circumference of each wheel were increased by 1 yard, the fore wheel would only make 4 revolutions more in going the same distance.

EXAMINATION XIII.

1. Reduce $\dfrac{ac + by + ay + bc}{af + 2bx + 2ax + bf}$.

2. Factor and reduce $(x^2 + 5xy + y^2)^2 - (x^2 - xy + y^2)^2$.

3. Solve $\begin{cases} x + y - z = 17 \\ y + z - x = 13 \\ z + x - y = 7 \end{cases}$

4. Solve $\begin{cases} x + \sqrt{xy} + y = 19 \\ x^2 + xy + y^2 = 133 \end{cases}$

5. Find 3 consecutive numbers whose product is 48 times the middle number.

6. Solve $\begin{cases} x^{\frac{1}{2}} + y^{\frac{1}{2}} = 5 \\ x^{-\frac{1}{2}} + y^{-\frac{1}{2}} = \frac{5}{6} \end{cases}$

7. Product of $\sqrt{a + 2\sqrt{b}}$ and $\sqrt{a - 2\sqrt{b}}$.

EXAMINATION XIV.

1. Factor: $x^2 - 23x + 132$
   $a^2 + 2ab - c^2 + b^2$
   $8a^3 + 27y^3$
   $1 + 6mn + 9m^2n^2$
   $9x^2 - 16y^2 + 8y - 1$.

2. Find the values of x, y, z, and u in the equations:
   $x + y + z = 15$
   $x + y + u = 16$
   $x + z + u = 17$
   $y + z + u = 18$.

3. If the greater of two numbers be added to $\frac{1}{8}$ of the less, the sum will be 50, but if the less be divided by $\frac{1}{8}$ of the greater, the quotient will be 2; what are the numbers?

4. Solve $\dfrac{\sqrt{4x+1} + 2\sqrt{x}}{\sqrt{4x+1} - 2\sqrt{x}} = 9$

5. Given $x + \sqrt{a-x} = \dfrac{a}{\sqrt{a-x}}$, to find x.

6. Multiply $9\sqrt{3a} + 2$ by $2 - 9\sqrt{3a}$

7. Find the least common multiple of $a^3 - 8a^2 + 19a - 12$, $a^3 - 9a^2 + 26a - 24$, and $a^3 - 6a^2 + 11a - 6$.

8. The sum of two numbers is 124, and if the greater is divided by the less, the quotient is 4 and the remainder is 4. Find the numbers.

9. A person borrowed a certain sum of money on interest at 6 per cent.; in 13 years the interest amounted to $110 less than the sum loaned; what was the sum loaned?

10. (a) Add $\dfrac{x-y}{xy}$, $\dfrac{y-z}{yz}$ and $\dfrac{z-x}{xz}$

(b) Divide $\dfrac{x^2 - 5x + 6}{x+4}$ by $\dfrac{x-2}{x^2 + x - 12}$

(c) Add $\dfrac{a}{a^2+1}$, $\dfrac{a^2}{1-a^2}$ and $\dfrac{a^4}{a^4-1}$

Note—Any five of the ten.

EXAMINATION XV.

1. Factor the following quantities:
(1.) $121 a^2 + 81 y^2 + 198 a y$.
(2.) $64 x^2 - 4 y^2$.
(3.) $a^6 - b^6$.

2. Did you follow any general laws in factoring these quantities? If so, state them.

3. Solve the following equations:

(1.) $\dfrac{x-16}{18} - \dfrac{17-4x}{9} = \dfrac{5x}{7} - \dfrac{4-26x}{32-17x} - \dfrac{3x}{14}$

(2.) $\dfrac{x}{a+b} + \dfrac{y}{a-b} = \dfrac{1}{a-b}$

(3.) $\dfrac{x}{a+b} - \dfrac{y}{a-b} = \dfrac{1}{a+b}$

4. Extract the square root of $2x^5 + 3x^2 + x^6 + 1 - 2x - x^4$.

5. Find the numerical value of $\sqrt{y}\,(\sqrt{y^3-x} - 3x^{-2} - xy^0)$ when $x = 2$ and $y = 3$.

6. Solve the following problems:

a. If the floor of a hall had been 9 feet wider and 4 feet longer it would have contained 137 square yards more, and if it had been 2 feet less in width and 1 foot less in length it would have contained 272 square feet less; how many square yards in the hall?

b. I paid $34.50 for corn at 75 cts., wheat at $1, and oats at 50 cts. a bushel. I sold ⅔ of the corn and ½ of the wheat at 50 per cent. advance, gaining on the corn ⅔ as much as on the wheat, and on the sale the cost of the oats. How many bushels of each did I buy?

7. Explain the law of exponents in multiplication. The law of signs.

EXAMINATION XVI.

1. Resolve the following into prime factors:

$a^{2n} - c^{2n}$; $a^4 - 6a^2c + 9c^2$; $m^6 - 12m^3 - 13$; $ad + d - 2a - 2$.

2. The sum of M's and N's money is a dollars and their difference is b dollars; how many dollars has each?

3. Given $am - b - \dfrac{ax}{b} + \dfrac{x}{m} = o$ to find x.

4. R and S laid a wager of $20; if R loses, he will have as much as S will then have; if S loses, he will have half of what R will then have; find the money of each.

5. Given $\begin{Bmatrix} x + \sqrt{(x\,y)} + y = 9 \\ x^2 + x\,y + y^2 = 27 \end{Bmatrix}$ to find x and y.

6. A merchant sold some cloth for $24, and some silk at $1 less a yard for the same sum; required the number of yards of each provided there were 2 yards of silk more than of cloth.

7. Expand $(c^2 - c^{-2})^6$ by the binomial theorem.

8. Suppose a body moves 12 feet the first second, 6 feet the next second, 3 feet the next second, and so on until it stops; what is the entire distance it can reach?

EXAMINATION XVII.

1. Define monomial, polynomial, elimination, radical, quadratic. Write a homogeneous trinomial of the fourth degree, with the second term negative.

2. Write the theorems applicable to composition and factoring.

3. The fraction whose numerator is $2x$ plus 4 and whose denominator is 3, minus the fraction whose numerator is x minus 3 and whose denominator is 4, equals the fraction whose numerator is x plus 2 and whose denominator is 3 plus $3\tfrac{1}{3}$. Find the value of x.

4. Illustrate each method of elimination by solutions of the following problem: $5x$ plus $2y$ equals 41, $3x$ minus $4y$ equals 9.

5. Derive and state the law of signs in the binomial theorem; the law of exponent; the law of coefficients.

6. Find the value, in simplest form, of the following: Two times the square root of 3; three times the square root of $\tfrac{1}{3}$; four times the fourth root of 32, minus four times the fourth root of $\tfrac{1}{8}$; two times the square root of $\tfrac{1}{5}$, multiplied by two times the square root of $\tfrac{5}{8}$; twelve, divided by the square root of three.

7. What is the general form of an affected quadratic equation? State the different methods of completing the square.

FINAL EXAMINATION QUESTIONS.

8. Find the value of x and y in the following: x squared plus y squared equal 208; x plus y equal 20?

9. A square field contains ¼ as many acres as there are rods in the fence inclosing it; what is the length of the fence?

10. There is a fraction whose numerator diminished by 5, and the denominator by the numerator the value is ¼. but if the numerator be increased by the denominator and the denominator by 33, its value is ½. What is the fraction?

EXAMINATION XVIII.

1. Name and define symbols of operation. Define similar and dissimilar terms, homogeneous terms, binomial, trinomial and polynomial.

2. Derive the binomial theorem.

3. Derive the formulas of arithmetical progression.

4. There are three numbers, whose sum is 156; the second is $3\frac{1}{2}$ times the first, and the third is equal to the remainder left, after subtracting the difference of the first and second from 100. Required the numbers.

5. A person bought two cubical stacks of hay for £41, each of which cost as many shillings per cubic yard as there were yards in the side of the other, and the greater stood on more ground than the less by 19 square yards. What was the price of each?

EXAMINATION XIX.

1. Write a trinomial with 2d term negative, and twice the product of the other terms, also a homogeneous trinomial of 5th degree.

2. Write all the factors of 66.

3. Discuss fully "the binomial theorem."

4. $\dfrac{3}{1-2x} - \dfrac{7}{1+2x} + \dfrac{4-20x}{1-4x} =$ what?

ALGEBRA. 161

5. Find all the values of x in $2x + 2px = q$.

6. A certain fraction is equal to $\frac{1}{3}$ when its numerator is increased by 1, and $\frac{1}{4}$ when its denominator increased by 1. Find it.

7. Work by all the methods known to you
$4x + 3y = 48$
$5y - 3x = 22$

8. The sum of two numbers is a, and the sum of their cubes is 34a; find the numbers.

EXAMINATION XX.

1. Prove $-a$ multiplied by $-b =$ plus ab.

2. Divide ax raised to $(m-2n)$th power by a raised to $-n$th power multiplied by x raised to $(m-n)$th.

3. Prove x raised to a power indicated by $-2 =$ one over x square.

4. Factor: $a^{4n} - b^{4n}$.

5. Write the value of a raised to $2n$th power over b raised to the nth power, integral form.

6. If a is to b as c is to d, prove am is to bn as cm is to dn.

7. Derive formula for S. in geometrical progression.

8. $\frac{4}{5}$ of the square root of a over c divided by $\frac{2}{3}$ of the cube root of a over c.

9. Find the square root of a over 3 multiplied by the cube root of a over 3.

10. $(x$ plus $4)$ squared $- 6$ times the square root of $(x - 4) = 16$ over $x - 4$, to find x.

EXAMINATION XXI.

1. Define algebra, root, evolution, index, surd.

2. Remove the parenthesis from the following expression and reduce the result:
$4x^3 - 2x^2 - [x^2 - (6x^2 + 5x - 7) - 6x + 1]$
66

3. Find the factors of $x-y$.

11

4. $\left.\begin{array}{l}\dfrac{2}{x}+\dfrac{3}{y}-\dfrac{4}{z}=1\tfrac{1}{12}\\[4pt]\dfrac{3}{x}-\dfrac{4}{y}+\dfrac{5}{z}=1\tfrac{9}{24}\\[4pt]-\dfrac{4}{x}+\dfrac{5}{y}+\dfrac{6}{z}=\tfrac{1}{2}\end{array}\right\}$

5. Find the value of $b(8a^6b)^{\frac{1}{3}}+4a(a^3b^4)^{\frac{1}{3}}-(125a^6b^4)^{\frac{1}{3}}$.

6. The difference of two numbers is 4, and the sum of their squares is 208, what are the numbers?

7. $x^3 + y^3 = 407.$
$x + y = 11.$

8. Two numbers are to each other as 3 to 2, and if 6 be added to the greater and subtracted from the less the result will be as 3 to 1; what are the numbers?

9. Write formula to find S, in geometrical progression.

10. Write formula to find S in arithmetical progression.

16. ENGLISH LITERATURE.

At Least a Fourteen Weeks' Course, Including a Thorough Study of Four English Classics.

ENGLISH LITERATURE.

EXAMINATION I.

1. Name the books or parts of books you have read within the last two years.
2. Why is Dickens a popular novelist? Why are his works standard?
3. Name three American historians; three living poets. Give the title of one of the best productions of each.
4. Write an outline of one of Shakespeare's plays. Give a short quotation from it.
5. Name three productions of the "Age of Milton;" of the "Elizabethan Age;" of the "Ageof Johnson;" name a Greek author; a Latin author; a French author; a German author.

EXAMINATION II.

1. Name the different periods of English literature, and give a characteristic writer of each period.
2. Give the author of the following: (1) The Spectator, (2) The Faerie Queen, (3) The Deserted Village, (4) Thanatopsis, (5) The Autocrat of the Breakfast Table.
3. Give a production of each of the following: (1) Edgar A. Poe, (2) J. G. Holland, (3) Will Carleton, (4) Gen. Lew. Wallace, (5) Walter Scott.
4. Name three prominent American historians, three novelists, three poets and three essayists.
5. Give two quotations.

EXAMINATION III.

1. What can you say of Sir Walter Scott as a novelist? As a poet?
2. Name six of the most prominent American prose writers, and at least one production of each.

3. Write a full list of the books you have read within the last two years.

4. Take one of the books you have named and write your impressions of it.

5. Name the leading periodicals of to-day. A few of the papers of special literary value.

6. Write an outline for composition upon one of Shakespeare's plays, or write out at least a part of the composition.

EXAMINATION IV.

1. What are the ages of English and American literature.

2. Who in America were contemporary with Addison, Burns, Scott, Dickins?

3. Who wrote Tam O'Shanter, John Gilpin, Ivanhoe, Vanity Fair, Uncle Tom's Cabin, Robert Elsmere? Who wrote the criticism of Elsmere?

4. Name your favorite authors and state why you deem their productions specially elevating in their character.

5. Tell me not in mournful numbers,
"Life is but an empty dream!"
For the soul is dead that slumbers,
And things are not what they seem.

6. (a) Explain the term "mournful numbers."

   (b) Why is the second line enclosed by quotation marks? Is the expression, "Life is but an empty dream," a rhetorical figure? If so, what figure is it?

   (c) Scan the first line, and name metre employed.

   (d) Who wrote this? In what poem?

EXAMINATION V.

1. Give briefly the origin of the English language and the leading characteristics of the Normans and the Saxons.

2. Enumerate the influences that lead to the Elizabethan literature. Mention the four stages of Shakespeare's mental development perceptible and the principal writings of each period.

3. Name five English historians and five novelists with a work of each.

4. Give the difference between the critical and the creative style of composition.

5. Mention several peculiarities of Goldsmith, Cowper, Pope, Coleridge.

6. Name some of Tennyson's powers, of Brayant's, of Whittier's, of Holmes'.

7. State the periods into which American literature may be divided and name the characteristics of each.

8. Tell what you can about the life and writings of Washington Irving.

9. Who wrote (a) The Canterbury Tales, (b) Samson Agonistes, (c) Rape of the Lock, (d) The Deserted Village, (e) Prisoner of Chillon, (f) Thanatopsis, (g) Gold Foil, (h) Hoosier Schoolmaster, (i) Prince of India.

10. Tell what you can of the progress of American literature and its present outlook.

EXAMINATION VI.

1. Define and give derivation of word "language," and state theories concerning origin of language.

2. Give origin of English language and discuss briefly effect of Norman conquest upon the same.

3. Name five American and five English authors, and a production from pen of each—designating one modern American and one modern English novelist.

4. Name the different departments of literature, designate and discuss one favorite poem.

5. What can you say of the progress of American literature?

EXAMINATION VII.

1. About how old is English literature said to be?
2. Name three writers detween Chaucer and Elizabeth.
3. To what characteristics and works does Milton owe his prominence?
4. Who wrote Lycidas, Cato, Much Ado About Nothing, Village Blacksmith, Vicar of Wakefield, Spectator, Prisoner of Chillon, Guy Mannering, Tam O'Shanter, Robinson Crusoe.
5. Thomas Gray lived when and where?
   (a) Mention five facts in his personal character.
   (b) Mention four of his contemporaries.
   (c) Name any of his writings.
   (d) What is an elegy?

EXAMINATION VIII.

The poem by Bret Harte, entitled "Dickens in Camp," was given to the class, with the following questions:

1. What does the subject mean?
2. Paraphrase each stanza, beginning with the first, and proceeding in order given.
3. Write three sentences of the poem that are to be understood literally, and three figuratively

(165)

17. LATIN.

Cæsar Through the Helvetian War

LATIN.

EXAMINATION I.

1. Give the cause of the Helvetian war.
2. Give in brief the life of Caesar.
3. Translate: Itaque rem suscipit et a Sequanis impetrat ut per fines suos Helvetios ire patiantur obsidesque uti inter sese dent perficit; Sequani, ne itinere Helvetios prohibeant; Helvetii, ut sine maleficio et injuria a transeant. Divico respondit: Ita Helvetios a majoribus suis institutos esse, uti obsides accipere non dare consuerint ejus rei populum Romanum esse testem.
4. Dumnorigem ad se vocat, fratrem adhibet, quae in eo reprehendat, ostendit, quae ipse intellegat, quae civitas queratur, proponit; monet ut in reliquum tempus omnes suspitiones vitet; praeterita se Diviciaco fratri condonare dicit. Dumnorigi custodes ponit, ut quae agat quibuscum loquatur, scire possit.
5. Give the construction of Helvetios, patiantur, prohibeant, transeant, quae, vitet, fratri, loquatur, and scire.
5. What is the construction of Ita Helvetios, etc.—esse testem. Apply the rule to the same.

EXAMINATION II.

1. Translate "Et id conspicati Helvetii, qui in montem sese receperant, rursus instare et proelium redintegrare coeperunt. Romani conversa signa bipartito intulerunt: prima et secunda acies, ut victis ac summotis resisteret; tertia, ut venientes sustineret."
2. Explain the use of redintegrare; the case of acies, victis, tertia, and explain the mode of resisteret.

3. Translate "Item Allobroges qui trans Rhodanum vicos possessionesque habebant, fuga se ad Caesarem recipiunt, et demonstrant sibi praeter agri solum nihil esse reliqui."

4. Explain the use of esse; the case of fuga, sibi, reliqui.

5. Give principal parts of verbs in both voices if possible; redintegrare, coeperunt, habebant, didicisse, venientes.

6. How are negative results expressed? Illustrate.

7. How is duration of time expressed? Illustrate.

EXAMINATION III.

1. Write a sketch of Julius Caesar.

2. Translate and parse italicised words: Caesari cum id nuntiatum esset, *eos* per provinciam nostram iter facere *conari*, maturat ab urbe proficisci, et quam maximis potest *itineribus* in Galliam ulteriorem contendit, et ad Genuam pervenit. Provinciae toti quam maximum *potest* militum numerum imperat—erat omnino in Gallia ulteriore legio una; *pontem*, qui erat ad Genuam, *jubet* rescindi.

3. Name four words in English derived from words of the second question.

EXAMINATION IV.

1. Write a short biography of Caesar.

2. Gallia est omnis divisa in partes tres, quarum unam incolunt Belgae, aliam Aquitani, tertiam, qui ipsorum lingua Celta, nostra Galli appellantur. Gallos ab Aquitanis Garumna flumen a Belgis Matrona et Sequana dividit. Interea ea legione, quam secum habebat, militibusque, qui ex provincia convenerant, a lacu Lemanno, qui in flumen Rhodanum influit, ad montem Juram, qui fines Sequanorum ab Helvetiis dividit, milia passuum decem novem, murum in altitudinem pedum sedecim, fossamque perducit.

(a) Translate the above.
(b) Divisa est. Why not dividitur?
(c) Why not divisus est instead of divisa est?
(d) How do you account for the compound subject Matrona et Sequana having a singular verb.
(e) Quam, parse and decline to the vocative singular.
(f) Where is convenerant found?

EXAMINATION V.

1. Translate: Consuesse enim deos immortales, *quo* gravius homines ex commutatione rerum doleant, quos pro scelere eorum ulcisci velint, his secundiores interdum res et diuturniorem impunitatem *concedere*.

2. Helvetii cum omnibus suis carris secuti, impedimenta in *unum* locum contulerunt; ipsi confertissima acie, rejecto nostro equitatu, phalange facta, sub primam nostram aciem *successerunt*.

3. Ab eisdem nostra consilia, quaeque in *castris* gerantur, hostibus enuntiari; hos a se coerceri non posse.

4. Complures annos portoria reliqua que omnia Haeduorum vectigalia parvo pretio redempta habere, propterea quod illo licente contra liceri audeat nemo.

5. Parse the italicized words.

EXAMINATION VI.

1. What people used the Latin language? Who wrote Caesar, and what is it about?

2. Translate: His rebus[1] adducti et auctoritate Orgetorigis permoti, constituerunt ea[2] quae ad proficiscendum[3] pertinerent comparare; sementes quam maximas facere[4], ut in itinere[5] copia frumenti suppeteret.[6] Ad eas res[7] conficiendas[8] biennium sibi satis esse duxerunt.

3. Parse the numbered words.

EXAMINATION VII.

1. Divico respondit: Ita *Helvetios* a majoribus suis *institutos esse*, uti *obsides* accipere, non *dare* consuerint;

LATIN. 173

ejus *rei* populum Romanum esse *testem*. Hoc responso dato, discessit.

2. Write a translation of the above as nearly literal as the English idiom will allow.
3. Decline majoribus, rei, populum.
4. Give a synopsis of respondit, accipere, esse, dare.
5. Parse the words underscored.
6. Write two derivative English words from each of five Latin words given above, naming the Latin words taken in each instance.
7. Who were Divico, Helvetios, obsides, Populum Romanum, Caesar?
8. What were Caesar's commentaries?

EXAMINATION VIII.

1. What is declension?
2. How are the declensions distinguished from one another? Illustrate.
3. State general rules for declension of nouns.
4. What are the principal parts of a Latin verb? Illustrate each conjugation.
5. Name the irregular verbs and inflect one of them.
6. Translate the following:
7. Ad haec Ariovistus respondit:" Jus esse belli, ut qui vicessent, iis, quos vicissent, quem ad modum vellent, imperarent: item Populum Romanum victis non ad alterius praescriptum, sed ad suum arbitrium, imperare consuesse."
8. "Who was Ariovistus?"
9. Write the rule for case of iis, Populum and quos.
10. Parse imperarent and consuesse.

EXAMINATION IX.

1. Translate literally the following:
2. Post ejus mortem nihilo minus Helvetii id. quod constituerant facere conantur, ut e finibus suis exeant.

Ubi jam se ad eam rem paratos esse arbitrati sunt, oppida sua omnia, numero ad duodecim, vicos ad quadringentos. reliqua privata aedificia incendunt, frumentum omne praeterquam quod secum portaturi erant, comburunt, ut domum reditionis spe sublata, paratiores ad omnia pericula subeunda essent. Trium mensium molita cibaria sibi quemque domo efferre jubent.

3. Nihilo, part of speech, account for case; quod, parse and decline constituerant, principal parts and, where found; Conantur, reason for tense; numero, rule for case; ad, parse; vicos, decline; portaturi erant, where found; comburunt, principal parts; sublata, from what verb? What part of verb? Rule for use; sibi, rule for case; domo, rule for case; jubent, principal parts.

EXAMINATION X.

1. Interea ea legione, quam secum habebat, militibusque, qui ex provincia convenerant, a lacu Lemanno, qui in flumen Rhodanum influit, ad montem Juram, qui fines Sequanorum ab Helvetiis dividit, milia passuum decem novem murum, in altitudinem pedum sedecim, fossamque perducit. Eo opere perfecto praesidia disponit, castella communit, quo facilius, si se invito transire conarentur, probibere possit.

2. Legione, case and declension; quam, parse and decline; secum, explain form and name parts of speech; convenerant, principal parts and where found; lacu, decline; ad, parse; milia, form, case and rule; perducit, give form and construction; Eo, parse; se, rule for case; conarentur, where found, mood and tense.

EXAMINATION XI.

1. Perfacile factu esse, illis probat, conata perficere, propterea quod ipse suae civitatis imperium obtenturus esset: non esse dubium, quin totius Galliae plurimum Helvetii possent: se suis copiis suoque exercitu illis

regna conciliaturum, confirmat. Hac oratione adducti, inter se fidem et jusjurandum dant, et, regno occupato, per tres potentissimos ac firmissimos populos totius Galliae sese potiri posse sperant.

2. Hoc proelio facto, reliquas copias Helvetiorum ut consequi posset, pontem in Arare faciendum curat atque ita exercitum transducit. Helvetii, repentino ejus adventu commoti, cum id, quod ipsi diebus viginti aegerrime confecerant, ut flumen transirent uno illum die fecisse intellegerent, legatos ad eum mittunt: cujus legationis Divico princeps fuit, qui bello Cassiano dux Helvetiorum fuerat.

3. Parse:
   (1) Factu, conata, confirmat, regno, potiri.
   (2) Faciendum, repentino, Divico.

EXAMINATION XII.

1. Translate into English, and parse the italicized words:

2. Eodem die ab exploratoribus certior factus hostes sub monte consedisse milia *passuum* ab ipsius castris octo, qualis esset natura montis et qualis in circuitu ascensus, qui *cognoscerent*, misit. Renuntiatum est *facilem* esse.

EXAMINATION XIII.

1. Translate into Latin.
   (1.) He says that the Romans are going to storm (assault) the town.
   (2.) The soldiers can fight.
   (3.) The consul was in command of the legion.
   (4.) Let us occupy the city.
   (5.) Caesar's plans have been reported to the Germans by the Gauls.
   (6.) Orgetorix urges Casticus to seize the royal power.

2. Translate into English.
   (1.) Omnibus moriendum est.
   (2.) Haedus et Lupus.

(3.) Haedus, stans in tecto domus, lupo pratereunti maledixit. Cui lupus, Non tu, inquit, sed tectum mihi maledicit. Saepe locus et tempus homines timidos audaces reddit.

EXAMINATION XIV.

1. Translate:
   (1.) Interim cotidie Caesar Haeduous frumentum, quod essent publice polliciti, flagitare.
   (2) Nam propter frigora, quod Gallia sub septentrionibus (ut ante dictum est) posita est, non modo frumenta in agris matura non erant, sed ne pabuli quidem satis magna copia suppetebat: eo autem frumento, quod flumine Arare navibus subvexerat, propterea minus uti poterat, quod iter ab Arare Helvetii averterant, a quibus discedere nolebat.
   (3. (Diem ex die ducere Haedui: conferri, comportari, adesse, dicere.
2. Classify all the verbs according to their conjugations, giving only the form of the first person, singular, present indicative active.
3. Classify all the nouns according to their declensions, giving only the form of the nominative singular.
4. Give the construction, in order of Haeduos, frumentum, frigora, copia, frumento, flumine, iter.
5. Conjugate the present indicative of "nolebat."
6. Give reason for the form "conferri."

EXAMINATION XV.

Translate "Flumen est Arar, quod per fines Haeduorum et Sequanorum in Rhodanum influit incredibili lenitate, ita ut oculis, in utram partem fluat, judicari non possit.
1. Parse quod in full.
2. Decline flumen.

3. What other words in this extraction contain the same root as flumen?

4. Give the rule for the case of lenitate.

5. Give the principal parts of possit, and conjugate it in the indicative mood, present tense.

6. What are the component parts of this word?

7. Account for the mood of fluat.

EXAMINATION XVI.

1. What was the origin of the Helvetian war? How did it result?

2. Who was Divitiacus? Dumnorix? Labienus? Liscus?

3. Translate Postquam id animum advertit, copias suas Caesar in proximum collem subducit, equitatumque, qui sustineret hostium impetum, misit.

4. Explain case of id. Compare proximum. Sustineret, why subjunctive?

5. Translate Flumen est Arar, quod per fines Æduorum et Sequanorum in Rhodanum influit, incredibili lenitate, ita ut oculis, in utram partem fluat, judicari non possit.

6. Parse quod. Decline utram. Syntax of fluat.

7. Translate Divico respondit: "Ita Helvetios a majoribus suis institutos esse, uti obsides accipere, non dare consuerint; ejus rei populum Romanum esse testem."

8. Syntax of institutos. Decline obsides. Principal parts of accipere.

9. Translate Divitiacus, multis cum lacrimis Caesarem complexus, obsecrare coepit, ne quid gravius in fratrem statueret: "Scire se illa esse vera, nec quemquam ex eo plus quam se doloris capere."

10. Explain use of infinitives in indirect discourse. Parse quemquam. Conjugate capere in the perfect subjunctive active.

EXAMINATION XVII.

1. Translate and parse italicized words in full:
2. Hujus est civitatis longe amplissima auctoritas omnis orae maritimae *regionum* earum; quod et naves habent Veneti plurimas, *quibus* in Britanniam *navigare consuerunt* et *scientia* atque usu nauticarum rerum reliquos antecedunt, et in magno impetu maris atque *aperto* paucis portibus interjectis, quos tenent ipsi, omnes fere, qui eo mari uti consuerant, habent *vectigales*.

EXAMINATION XVIII.

1. Translate and parse italicized words in full:
2. Interea ea *legione,quam* secum habebat, militibusque, qui ex provincia *convenerant*, a lacu Lemanno, qui in flumen Rhodanum influit, ad montem Juram, qui fines Sequanorum ab Helvetiis dividit, *milia* passuum decem novem, murum in altitudinem *pedum* sedecim, fossamque perducit. Eo *opere* perfecto, praesidia disponit, castella communit, quo facilius, si se *invito* transire conarentur, prohibere possit.

EXAMINATION XIX.

1. Qui *cupidius novissimum* agmen insecuti alieno *loco*, cum equitatu Helvetiorum proelium committent; et pauci de nostris *cadunt*.
2. Translate and parse italicized words in full.

EXAMINATION XX.

1. Translate and parse the italicized words.
2. *Relinquebatur una* per Sequanos via, qua Sequanis invitis. Helvetii propter angustias *ire* non *poterant*.
3. Aedui cum *se* defendere non *possent, legatos* ad Caesarem *mittunt rogatum auxilium*.
4. Cæsar, Equitatum omnem praemittit,*qui videant* quas in *partes hostes, iter faciant*.

LATIN. 179

EXAMINATION XXI.

1. Decline lacrima-ae, lacus-us, fides-ei, homo inis, dominus, i, flumen, inis.
2. Compare bonus, potens, superus, facilis, inferus.
3. Decline bonus in three genders.
4. Give a synopsis of dico in the indicative.
5. Translate and parse underscored words: Apud *Helvetios* longe nobilissimus et ditissimus fuit Orgetorix, is *conjurationem* nobilitatis fecit et *civitati* persuasit ut de finibus suis cum omnibus copiis exirent.

EXAMINATION XXII.

Translate into good English: Diem ex die ducere Aedui; conferri, comportari, adesse, dicere. Ubi *se* diutius duci intellexit et diem instare, quo die *frumentum* militibus metiri oporteret; *convocatis* eorum principibus, quorum magnam copiam in castris habebat, in his Diviaco et Lisco, qui summo *magistratui* praeerat (quem *Vergobretum* appellant Aedui, qui creatur *annuus*, et vitae necisque in suos habet potestatem), graviter eos accusat, quod, cum neque emi neque ex agris sumi posset, tam necessario *tempore*, tam propinquis *hostibus*, ab iis non sublevetur; praesertim cum magna ex parte eorum precibus *adductus* bellum susceperit: multo etiam gravius, quod *sit destitutus*, queritur.

EXAMINATION XXIII.

1. Analyze the first sentence and explain the construction of ducere, conferri and dicere.
2. Give reasons for the infinitives duci and instare in second sentence. When is the subject of an infinitive in the nominative case?
3. Parse the words italicized and give the rule of syntax in each instance.
4. Explain the use of oporteret, and show in what respect the use of this verb is limited.

5. Write out in full the principal parts of metiri, name its subject and mention the class of verbs to which it belongs.

6. Derivation of principibus; does its case imply time, cause or concomitant?

7. How is castris governed? When is in followed by the accusative? When by the ablative?

8. What case does praeerat govern, and is the present instance an example of such use?

9. Explain the use of quod in the indicative and subjunctive moods respectively.

10. Outline the life of Caesar, and name the Roman consuls during the period of which the above selection is an account.

18. PSYCHOLOGY.

Embracing the Intellect, Sensibilities and Will.

PSYCHOLOGY.

EXAMINATION I.

1. Give three reasons why the teacher should study psychology.
2. Give a summary of the knowing activities.
3. Define (1) sensation, (2) perception, (3) percept, (4) sensorium.
4. What are the charteristics of intuitive truths?
5. Illustrate the use of the imagination.
6. State the primary laws of association, the secondary laws of association.
7. What is the difference between the implicit and the explicit form of reasoning?
8. What is the relation of feeling to morals?
9. What is the difference between self-love and selfishness.
10. What is the will and what arguments support its freedom?

EXAMINATION II.

1. Show that perception is the foundation of knowledge.
2. By what power do you know the color of an orange? By what power do you know the substance of an orange? By what power do you know that you know it?
3. What are the most important steps in cultivating memory?
4. Give and name an inductive syllogism, a deductive syllogism; name the elements in one.
5. What are the thinking faculties?

PSYCHOLOGY. 183

6. What powers are the sources of original knowledge?
7. What is the relation of the feeling to the intellect and to the will?
8. Define, classify, and enumerate forms of love.
9. What are motives.
10. How can you cultivate will power?

EXAMINATION III.

1. What are the leading faculties of the mind and their respective functions?
2. How does the study of psychology aid the teacher in his work?
3. When you wish to determine any of the properties of matter, or space, or distance, what faculties of the mind do you employ?
4. Define memory, imagination, intuition, consciousness, reasoning, sensibility.
5. What means may be employed to strengthen the memory? To cultivate attention? Imagination?

EXAMINATION IV.

1. Define intellect, science.
2. Classify the intellectual powers. Define two.
3. What power enables us to form ideals?
4. Give the steps in forming a conception.
5. What is thinking?
6. How do we get the idea of time?
7. Classify the desires, and show why they are important.
8. Define conscience, and give characteristics.
9. Give the will powers in order of activity.
10. What makes a moral man?

EXAMINATION V.

1. Define science, mind, intellect, sensibilities, will.
2. Name the powers of perception.
3. What knowledge do these give us?

4. What would be the effect if they all were absent at birth?

5. What is the effect upon those remaining if some are lost?

6. If all the perceptive powers were cultivated to the highest degree, how would this affect memory, imagination, conception, judgment, the aesthetic power.

7. What training is afforded to the several senses by school work?

8. What is reasoning?

9. How are emotions awakened?

10. Does the training of the will require the breaking of the will?

EXAMINATION VI.

1. Define emotions, affections and desires.

2. What has the will to do with the cultivation of the habit of attention.

3. What branches in the common school curriculum are well adapted for the training of judgment? Why?

4. What use is made of the imagination in the acquisition of a knowledge of geography?

5. Give rules or methods for the cultivation of the perceptive powers.

6. By what law of association do you remember names? Explain.

EXAMINATION VII.

1. Define mind, psycholgy.

2. Prove the existence of mind as distinct from matter.

3. What is sense perception?

4. By what power do we know substance?

5. Give the laws of memory and illustrate two.

6. What are the sub-divisions of the comparative power, and what is its office?

7. Give an analysis of the sensibilities.

8. Distinguish consciousness from conscience.
9. What makes an act one for which we are responsible.
10. Prove that you are a free agent.

EXAMINATION VIII.

1. Define intellect, science.
2. Classify the intellectual powers. Define two.
3. What power enables us to form ideals?
4. Give the steps in forming a conception.
5. What is thinking?
6. How do we get the idea of time?
7. Classify the desires, and show why they are important.
8. Define conscience, and give characteristics.
9. Give the powers in order of activity.
10. What makes a moral man?

EXAMINATION IX.

1. Define automatic action, reflex, instinctive, voluntary.
2. What are the characteristics of necessary ideas?
3. Are intuitions particular notions, or general?
4. Give a syllogism—indicate the terms, the premises.
5. Give an example of inductive and one of deductive reasoning.
6. Are you a free agent? Give reasons.
7. What is the difference between a stubborn man and one of great will power?

EXAMINATION X.

1. How do we know that mind exists?
2. What is the difference between a sensation and a perception?
3. Explain the philosophy of the perceptive process.
4. What is generalization? Give an example.
5. Name the different kinds of truth and state their differences.

6. Show how we reason, and state the principal laws that govern the process of reasoning.

7. Prove the existence of primary or first truths.

8. How do we obtain an idea of space?

9. Explain the terms, subjective and objective as used in mental philosophy.

10. Explain the fundamental differences between the intellect, the sensibilities, and the will.

EXAMINATION XI.

1. Prove that the consciousness is not a distinct faculty.

2. Give what you consider the most plausible theory of perception.

3. To what limitations is all knowledge derived from the senses subject?

4. What is the difference between a necessary and a contingent truth?

5. Run the line between the brute and the human intellect, showing wherein they differ.

6. Analyze the conscience, showing in what respect it belongs to the intellect and in what respect to the sensibilities.

7. Account for the idea of cause.

EXAMINATION XII.

1. Show how we come by three forms of mental activity.

2. Is consciousness a distinct faculty of the mind? Give reasons.

3. Distinguish between sensation and perception.

4. Upon what does a talent for description of objects depend? Explain.

5. Is it possible by a voluntary effort to recall what has gone from the mind? If so, explain process.

6. Explain probable reasoning, and give an example.

7. Does civilization promote patriotism? Explain.

PSYCHOLOGY. 187

EXAMINATION XIII.

1. Nature of attention and methods of cultivating the same.
2. Nature of perception and methods of cultivating the same.
3. Explain the inductive method of teaching, with examples.
4. Explain, on psychological grounds, the necessity of the study of mathematics.

EXAMINATION XIV.

1. How does mind differ from matter?
2. General classes of mental faculties.
3. Discriminate between sensation and perception.
4. Why do men use language and animals do not, both having an equal number of senses?

EXAMINATION XV.

1. Name three grand phases of mental life and show how they are connected with the primary and secondary powers of mind.
2. Explain and illustrate the difference between the subjective and objective.
3. By what faculty or faculties does a child acquire concrete knowledge? Abstract ideas.
4. How are our specific conceptions of soul and body formed?
5. What are the leading characteristics of imaginative thought?
6. Prove the existence of primary truths.
7. What are some of the causes that give rise to the sentiment of patriotism, and what effect has civilization on that sentiment.

EXAMINATION XVI.

1. Define abstraction, analogy, classification, generalization.
2. Write not less than one nor more than two pages on the importance of mental science.
3. Discuss the different forms of mental activity.
4. Distinguish between attention and thought.
5. Give an analysis of the perceptive process.
6. What do we mean by the primary qualities of bodies?
7. What is implied in an act of memory?
8. Give methods for the cultivation of memory.
9. How may the imagination be improved or strengthened?
10. How is the will related to other powers of the mind?

EXAMINATION XVII.

1. What is the difference between sensation and perception?
2. Distinguish between automatic, reflex and voluntary action.
3. Name five laws of memory or mental reproduction.
4. From what sources does imagination draw its materials?
5. If the imagination combines its materials according to laws, name some of them.
6. Distinguish betwen fancy and imagination.
7. What departments of literature are most indebted to imagination; and of what use is imagination to the individual and to society?
8. Define motive, and name proper motives to be appealed to in training children.
9. Do actions result commonly from single or from combined motives? What does this fact suggest to the teacher?
10. Name the sub-divisions of the power of the will.

EXAMINATION XVIII.

1. Define judgment. What is the relation of a good memory to sound judgment?
2. Which of the senses should be utilized in learning to spell? Give reasons for your views on this question.
3. Give three instances of the asociation of ideas by the law of similarity and three instances illustrating the association of ideas by contrast.
4. What value has the imagination for the student of history?
5. Give your plan for the cultivation of the emotions, affections and desires.
6. Give a synopsis of the mental powers.

EXAMINATION XIX.

1. Explain the functions of the perceptive powers.
2. What is the difference between the primary and secondary qualities of bodies.
3. Show how conception differs from perception.
4. Explain the different kinds of reasoning.
5. How does imagination influence culture?
6. How many memories has the mind? Give examples.
7. Does good reasoning ever lead to false conclusions? Give reasons for answer.
8. What are the primary intellectual faculties.

EXAMINATION XX.

1. Prove that psychology is a science.
2. How does the mind differ from matter?
3. Define the terms subjective, objective, analysis, synthesis, induction and deduction.
4. What is the difference between the primary and the secondary qualities of matter?
5. Explain how we reason.
6. Name the different kinds of truths and explain their differences.
7. How does the memory differ from the imagination?

EXAMINATION XXI.

1. Define consciousness, abstraction, perception, classification, association, theory, hypothesis.
2. Discuss mental science as a study and show its relation to other sciences.
3. Distinguish between mental reproduction and mental recognition.
4. Define reasoning from analogy and show its value.
5. What is your theory as to the "modus operandi" of the memory?
6. How do we recognize and distinguish first truths from all others?
7. Discuss the origin of our moral ideas and perceptions.
8. In what sense is the teacher born?

EXAMINATION XXII.

1. Classify and define the intellectual powers.
2. In what order do the different faculties of the mind develop?
3. State what is implied in an act of memory.
4. How would you strengthen the memory?
5. In what way can the imagination be cultivated?
6. Define affection, desire, passions.
7. State what is meant by the subjective and objective.
8. Explain the primary laws of association and state in what order they come into play in the child's mind.
9. Is there any agreement between the science of mind and the science of matter?

EXAMINATION XXIII.

1. Why should a teacher study mental philosophy.
2. Distinguish between presentative and representative power.
3. What is implied in an act of memory, and how can we cultivate the power thereof?

4. Give the different kinds of categorical propositions, with the signs of the same, and an example of each with its proper sign.

EXAMINATION XXIV.

1. Explain and illustrate the difference between the subjective and the objective.
2. How does the activity of the imagination manifest itself in childhood?
3. By what exercises are the perceptive powers cultivated?
4. State the primary laws of association and tell the order in which they come into play as the child develops.
5. Explain and illustrate the difference between contingent and necessary truths.

EXAMINATION XXV.

1. Give a general analysis of the mental powers.
2. Give an analysis of the perceptive process.
3. Define the organs of sense, and the amount of information derived from each.
4. Give the nature of mental reproduction, and the laws regulating it.
5. Give an analysis of the syllogism, and its laws.
6. What is the value of psychological knowledge to the teacher?

(192)

19. METHODS OF INSTRUCTION.

This includes a Discussion of the Principles of Education, Primary Definitions and Methods of Teaching the Common Branches.

METHODS OF INSTRUCTION.

EXAMINATION I.

1. Give the succesive steps in the subjective or inductive treatment of a subject and the objects attained by it. Also the subjective and deductive process.

2. What do you include in the term teaching? What general principles govern the art of teaching?

3. Would you teach manners and morals in school? If so, when and how?

4. What do you regard as the chief incentives to study? In what ways can you impress the minds of your pupils with the importance of education and culture?

5. Discuss school government, penalties and rewards, organization, classification.

EXAMINATION II.

1. What is the difference between proving knowledge and testing knowledge?

2. What is the object, and what should be the limit of language lessons?

3. How should spelling be taught in the advanced grades?

4. How should penmanship be taught?

5. What if a pupil refuses to study geography, or the parent refuses to provide a book?

6. What should be the temperature of a school room, in degrees?

7. What should be the length of a session of a primary school with and without recess?

METHODS OF INSTRUCTION. 195

EXAMINATION III.

1. Name some uses of the recitation.
2. What is "drill" and when is it to be employed?
3. What objects should the teacher have in view in teaching penmanship? Outline a good method?
4. Distinguish between language lessons and grammar, and state when the latter should be commenced.
5. How is moral training to be secured?

EXAMINATION IV.

1. Define pedagogy, teaching.
2. What is a kindergarten, and what special objects are sought through it?
3. Distinguish between a kindergarten and a primary school.
4. Generally speaking, what is the kindergarten period of childhood? The primary? The intermediate? The high school period?
5. What is the proper use of a text-book in geography, and what methods may a teacher properly employ to supplement it?

EXAMINATION V.

1. Have you any objections to teaching the alphabet as the first lessons in reading? If so, what?
2. How should the idea of number be developed in a child? May the concrete method be carried too far? If so, what is the limit?
3. When should technical grammar be taught? Why?
4. Give the steps in teaching the geography of Pennsylvania to an advanced class.
5. Name the essential conditions of good order in a school.
6. How many cubic feet of space should be allowed for each pupil in school?

EXAMINATION VI.

1. Distinguish between the science and the art of teaching.
2. Are there objections to making use of kindergarten methods in the public school? If so, what?
3. What are object lessons and what dangers attend them?
4. Name four important elements of governing power in the teacher.
5. Name four important conditions of good order in every school, not including the character of the teacher.
6. What will you do with an uninterested pupil? What with an uninteresting one?
7. Should text-books always be used? If not always, when should they not be used?

EXAMINATION VII.

1. Name and define the elements embraced in the problem of education.
2. Define culture and instruction and state clearly the difference between them.
3. Give not less than three general principles of education.
4. Define education, teaching, methods of culture, and methods of instruction and name the three general divisions embraced in each of the last two.
5. Name and define the different kinds of culture.
6. Perception: (1) Definition, (2) Importance of cultivation, (3) Methods of cultivating.
7. Attention under same heads.
8. Why should the teacher have a knowledge of the mind.
9. Define concrete and abstract instruction.
10. State what should be taught in childhood, or between the ages of five and ten years.

METHODS OF INSTRUCTION.   197

EXAMINATION VIII.

1. Define teaching as a science and as an art.
2. What is meant by a logical method in the work of teaching?
3. Describe the peculiar mental characteristics of a child six years of age.
4. On what principles is the kindergarten based?
5. What is the fundamental distinction between intellectual and moral education?
6. What are the limitations of exercise as a law of mental development?
7. Give an example of induction in teaching.
8. State how text-books can be used and how they can be abused.
9. What analogy exists between physical and mental digestion?
10. What is the ultimate end of school government?

EXAMINATION IX.

1. Define the science of teaching and name three of its leading principles.
2. By what methods may the reasoning powers be cultivated?
3. Distinguish between an empirical science and a rational science.
4. Give an example of synthesis in teaching.
5. Give the characteristics of good questions, and give examples
6. Who are the strongest opponents of public schools, and what is the ground of their opposition?

EXAMINATION X.

1. What I owe the profession.
2. Name five aids to good discipline.
3. Write six questions on the geography of our State.
4. Give an example of induction in teaching. Analysis.

5. Explain the difference between education and instruction.

6. Name and discuss three methods of conducting a recitation.

7. Revenues, institutes, school term in Pennsylvania.

8. Froebel, Pestalozzi, Mann, Page, Burrowes, Comenius, Parker.

EXAMINATION XI.

1. What are the leading characteristics of a good school?

2. Define education. Explain the relation and state the difference between knowledge and culture.

3. What general principles govern the art of teaching?

4. By what methods can a teacher cultivate in his pupils the ability to use language readily and accurately?

5. What methods may be employed by the teacher to awaken a proper spirit of investigation among his pupils?

6. What may be considered proper penalties in the government of a school?

7. What should be the chief reliance in securing and maintaining order?

8. What moral qualities should the teacher aim to cultivate in his pupils, and what means may be used to accomplish the object desired?

EXAMINATION XII.

1. Prove that there is an order of time in the development of the several intellectual faculties.

2. Give an example of inductive teaching and one of deductive.

3. Name and discuss four elements of governing power.

4. What are the advantages of classification in a school, and what are its disadvantages?

5. What principle should govern the administration of rewards and punishments in a school?

6. By what means would you cultivate originality in composition work?

METHODS OF INSTRUCTION. 199

EXAMINATION XIII.

1. Is uniformity of text-books necessary in arithemetic and geography? Why?
2. Discuss briefly the question of study after school hours for the purpose of discipline.
3. Discuss three characteristics of the true teacher.
4. Define school ethics.
5. What advantages and what disadvantages grow out of the division of a school into classes?
6. Why should little children be taught the concrete rather than the abstract?

NOTE—This list was headed Methods and School Management.

EXAMINATION XIV.

1. Define education, instruction, training. Explain the relation and state the difference between knowledge and culture.
2. What do you understand by the term methods, as applied to teaching? Illustrate by an example your method of teaching reading to beginners.
3. What is meant by discipline in the school?
4. How can the moral nature of pupils be most effectively aroused and strengthened by agencies at the disposal of the teacher?
5. What are the essential qualifications of a good teacher, natural and acquired?

EXAMINATION XV.

1. What was the central idea in the education of Athens? of Sparta?
2. Who was Socrates? Quintillian? Rousseau? Pestalozzi?
3. What are some of the leading principles advocated by Comenius?

4. Give a brief account of learning among the Saracens.
5. Who was Froebel? For what was he noted? What particular educational theories did he advance?

EXAMINATION XVI.

1. What do you conceive to be the principal purposes of school education?
2. Why is it important that the teacher should have a correct understanding of the objects of the educating process?
3. Name several of the important physical conditions of effective school work.
4. State two or more principles that a teacher should employ in arranging a programme of daily school work.
5. State your opinion of the relation of a knowledge of mental science to the art of instruction.
6. What faculties of the mind are the following subjects especially fitted to develop and strengthen—arithmetic, geography, history?
7. What are parochial schools? Technical schools? Nautical schools?
8. Name and locate four leading colleges in the state of Pennsylvania.

EXAMINATION XVII.

1. What constitutes an education?
2. Give four reasons to prove that teaching is a science.
3. What studies belong to childhood, to youth? Give reasons.
4. What are the characteristics of good advanced instruction?
5. How would you teach a pupil an idea? A thought? Illustrate.
6. Under what circumstances does the getting of knowledge give no discipline?

METHODS OF INSTRUCTION. 201

7. Show the significance of the personality of the teacher as a factor in education.
8. Give five incentives to study in the order of their value.
9. Why is it natural for a child's mind to pass from the concrete to the abstract in aquiring knowledge?
10. When was the common school system adopted? Name some of its early advocates.
11. Give, in round numbers, number of pupils, number of teachers, and entire cost of education for a year in state of Pennsylvania.

EXAMINATION XVIII.

1. By what method will you make the transition from a knowledge of oral speech to written language?
2. By what method will you pass the pupil from a simple knowledge of number to arithmetical calculation?
3. By what method will you teach any physical science, such as botany or ornithology?

EXAMINATION XIX.

1. Object lessons, their design, method and value.
2. The order of study as related to the various periods of school life.
3. Value of empirical sciences, and the order in which they should be taught.

EXAMINATION XX.

1. What is teaching?
2. Explain culture, instruction, training.
3. What are some of the proper incentives to study?
4. What is the great end of school training?
5. State why you consider teaching a profession?
6. What moral qualities should the teacher try to cultivate in his pupils?

7. What relation does the school hold to the state?

8. From your observation, what do you consider the greatest defects in our public school system?

EXAMINATION XXI.

1. Objects of the recitation.
2. Mistakes to be avoided in teaching primary reading.
3. Reasons in favor of oral spelling.
4. Inductive and deductive methods of reasoning as applied to teaching arithmetic.

EXAMINATION XXII.

1. What special preparation is necessary for the office of teaching?
2. Give the method of instruction in the elements of knowledge.
3. How will you impart instruction in what are termed empirical sciences?

20. HISTORY OF EDUCATION.

What is Included in a Work Like Painters, for Instance.

HISTORY OF EDUCATION.

EXAMINATION I.

1. What grand division contains the birth place of the human race?
2. What divisions may be made of the history of education?
3. What authority determines the character of education in China?
4. What influence controls the education of India?
5. Why is the education of Egypt called priestly education?
6. What was the ideal of Athenian education?
7. Name the three greatest thinkers of Athens.
8. Who was styled the Alexander of the intellectual world?
9. What three Romans exerted the greatest influence over the education of their period?
10. What effect had the advent of Christ upon education?
11. To what nation are we most indebted for our present civilization?
12. What were the seven liberal arts as taught in the monastic schools?
13. What was the object of the Crusades?
14. What three noted German humanists were born near the middle of the Fifteenth century?
15. What were the two underlying truths of the Reformation.
16. What date is the birth-day of the Reformation?

HISTORY OF EDUCATION. 205

17. Who was the leading educational reformer of the Sixteenth century?
18. What three names must be associated with his in the educational reform of this period?
19. Who were the Jesuists?
20. Name the two fundamental principles of Comenius.
21. Who wrote Emile?
22. Give the date and place of birth of Pestalozzi.
23. What were his leading works?
24. Who was Pestalozzi's most illustrious disciple?
25. Upon what does his fame chiefly rest?

EXAMINATION II.

1. It is said that education in the oriental nations does not develop a perfect man or woman. Why?
2. (a) What is caste education?
   (b) What nation is an example of caste education?
3. Distinguish between a theocratic and a priestly education.
4. Name five great educational reformers.
5. If history is a teacher, what lessons ought we to learn from the downfall of the Roman empire?
6. Name the causes that contributed in bringing about the revival of learning.
7. Give a brief account of the life and work of Froebel.
8. Upon what principles did Pestalozzi base his system?

EXAMINATION III.

1. What was the revival of learning?
2. State some of the educational principles of Pestalozzi.
3. Name and locate three of the greatest educational institutions in the United States.

EXAMINATION IV.

1. What benefit can a teacher derive from the history of education.
2. Who is the greatest teacher that ever lived?

3. Name three men that have left their impress upon pedagogy, and specify the benefit conferred by each.

4. What service was rendered by monasteries to education?

5. Name three facts in the history of education in Pennsylvania.

6. Give a brief outline of the time and influence of Charlemagne.

7. Give the general religion and political principles involved in the progress of the Reformation. Mention two political leaders (Reformation) two leaders in religious thoughts (Reformation).

EXAMINATION V.

1. How are schools free?

2. How, when, and where do teachers obtain their salary?

3. What is a school district?

4. Discuss taxes, appropriation, school directors, teachers and pupils.

5. (a) Name some of the leading educators of the day.
   (b) Some state superintendents.

6. What can you say of Colonel Parker?

NOTE—This list was headed School Law and History of Education.

EXAMINATION VI.

1. What are the Chinese classics?

2. What can you tell of the education of Egypt?

3. Tell what you know of Pythagoras.

4. Who was Socrates, and on what does his reputation depend?

5. Upon what does Luther's reputation as an educator rest?

6. Tell what you know of Comenius.

7. Compare humanism with philanthropinism.
8. Discuss Pestalozzi.
9. Compare English and French schools.
10. What is the condition of education to-day?

EXAMINATION VII.

1. What countries are known as the oriental nations? ancient classical nations?
2. What do you understand by the Reformation period? The Middle Ages?
3. What dates mark the limits of these periods?
4. Name two noted scholars of the Fifteenth century.
5. Name two prominent educational reformers of the Nineteenth century. Why were they noted?
6. What do you regard as the particular advantages of a public school system as compared with the systems of private or parochial schools?
7. What nations to-day occupy advanced educational positions?

EXAMINATION VIII.

1. Who was Socrates? When and where did he live and how did he die?
2. Name any peculiarities of his method, any of his famous pupils, and any lasting effect upon pedagogy produced by him.
3. What is meant by the Dark Ages?
4. What agencies chiefly produced the renaissance?
5. What evidence have we of Penn's interest in education?

EXAMINATION IX.

1. Write a page on Plato.
2. Give an account of the monitorial system of teaching as it prevailed in England and India.
3. Make a list of the five best books on education with which you are acquainted.

4. State the powers and duties of school directors in Pennsylvania.

5. Discuss the maxim: "From the known to the unknown."

EXAMINATION X.

1. The effort of Christianity in education.
2. The Reformation, and its relation to education.
3. Comenius, Froebel, Horace Mann, Parker, Wickersham.

21. NATURAL PHILOSOPHY.

An Amount Equivalent to What is Found in the Elementary Text-Book, Together With Laboratory Experiments.

NATURAL PHILOSOPHY.

EXAMINATION I.

1. Name and define five general properties of matter and illustrate each with some common example.

2. How do you find the velocity of a falling body at the end of any second? What will be the velocity of a body after it has fallen 4 seconds? How far will it fall in 4 seconds?

3. Define specific gravity. A stone weighs 12 lbs. in air and 10 lbs. in water: find the specific gravity.

4. Define weight. At what distance above the earth would a man weighing 225 lbs. at the surface, weigh 100 lbs.?

5. Explain two classes of levers. A lever of the second class is 20 ft. long: at what distance from the fulcrum must a weight of 80 lbs. be placed in order that it may be sustained by a power of 60 lbs.?

6. By means of a diagram explain the principle of the siphon.

7. Name and define the three ways in which heat can be distributed.

8. Give the name and effect of different kinds of mirrors. Of different kinds of lenses.

9. Discuss the construction and use of lightning rods.

EXAMINATION II.

1. Name and illustrate five universal properties of matter.

2. A body is thrown downward with an initial velocity of 10 feet per second; give (1) distance it falls in 4 seconds, (2) the distance it falls the fourth second, and (3) the velocity at the end of the fourth second. Give formula.

3. A system of three movable and three fixed pulleys, with cord attached to movable block, acts upon a weight resting on an inclined plane in a direction parallel to the plane which is 15 feet long and 3 feet high. Give relation of power to weight.

4. Explain latent heat and illustrate in the case of ice, water and steam.

5. Explain the modes of heat.

6. Describe and explain voltaic cell.

7. On what do the three elements of sound, intensity, pitch, and quality depend?

8. Construct an image for an object lying between the principal focus and twice the focal distance of a double convex lens.

EXAMINATION III.

1. Define matter, body and molecule.

2. What are the general or universal properties of matter? What the specific?

3. Mention the difference between a solid, a liquid, and a gas.

4. What is the great law of gravitation? Illustrate.

5. How may be found the specific gravity of a solid lighter than water?

6. Name the six elementary forms of all machines.

7. Of what does hydrostatics treat? What of the law of pressure?

8. Describe the Leyden jar, and define electrolysis.

9. What is light? Define the "wave" theory of light.

10. What are the sources of heat? Define specific heat; and what are the three ways in which it may be transferred from one body to another.

EXAMINATION IV.

1. Name and define the most important properties of matter both general and specific.

2. Distinguish betwen magnetic and electric attraction and repulsions. Give theory for electricity; for magnetism.

3. Describe the force pump, giving the laws of fluids illustrated.

4. Point out the changes in form of energy from the furnace fire through a high pressure engine to the heated axles set in motion.

5. (a) What physical force is due to the fact that wetting a rope shortens it? (b) A stone thrown over a tree reaches the ground 100 feet from where it was thrown in three seconds. How high did the stone go?

EXAMINATION V.

1. Define mass, molecule and atom.
2. What is a solid? a liquid? an æriform body?
3. Define gravitation and give the law or laws.
4. Name the six elementary forms of machines and give law of the screw.
5. With what velocity must a body be thrown upward to ascend 144 feet. Give 3d law of falling bodies.
6. Draw a diagram of the force pump and explain its action.
7. State the difference between frictional and voltaic electricity.
8. Name and define the different kinds of magnets.
9. Define heat and state the ways in which it may be transferred from one body to another.
10. Define solar spectrum and give laws of refraction of light.

EXAMINATION VI.

1. What is matter? A molecule?
2. Is matter indestructible?
3. How does molecular action differ in solids, liquids and gases?

4. Give a familiar example of a lever of the first kind, second and third kind, and show their operation.

5. What is acoustics?

6. How do solid, liquid and æriform bodies compare as conductors of sound?

7. Define heat and classify its effect on bodies. State the ways by which heat is transferred.

8. What is a siphon? State its uses. Define cohesion and adhesion.

9. Name the six elementary forms of machines and give the law of the screw.

10. Why can we with a tube suck up water with the mouth?

11. Give the laws of the refraction of light, and name and define the different kinds of refractors.

12. Define electrolysis, galvanometer, electro-magnet.

13. Give the two definitions of sound, and state difference between noise and music.

14. In what ways can a permanent magnet be made?

EXAMINATION VII.

1. What is the special domain of natural philosophy? How is it related to chemistry?

2. State the laws of falling bodies.

3. Does it require more work to lift a barrel of flour into a wagon four feet high than to place it there by rolling it up a plank 12 feet long? Show why.

4. What is a siphon, and how does it apply to intermittent springs?

5. Name the several kinds of electrical batteries. Describe one of them.

6. Describe the process of electrotyping.

7. A shot is fired before a cliff and the echo heard in six seconds. The temperature is 15 degrees centigrade, find the distance of the cliff.

8. Explain the principles involved in the construction of a thermometer.

9. Define and illustrate refraction of light.

10. What is meant by correlation of energy? Illustrate.

EXAMINATION VIII.

1. Two forces of 5 lbs. and 16 lbs. act on a point, and their resultant is 19 lbs.; find the angle between the forces.

2. A bar 4 feet 6 inches long rests with its ends on two props, and a weight of 496 lbs. is suspended from the bar 20 inches from one of the props. Find the pressure on the props.

3. State and prove the principle of Archimedes concerning bodies placed in fluids. Explain why cork floats in water, stating all the forces which act on it.

4. Describe the single barrel air-pump, and explain its working. If a barometer be under the receiver, how will it be affected by working the pump?

5. State how you conceive sound to be propegated through the atmosphere; state also its velocity in air and in water respectively.

6. What are the two kinds of spectacles necessary for long and short sight? Explain how it is that they remedy these defects.

7. If you look into a concave spherical mirror, and are sufficiently close to it, you see an enlarged and upright image of your face, but when the mirror is sufficiently distant, the image which you see is diminished and inverted. Explain the formation of the two images.

EXAMINATION IX.

1. Define *mass, atom, molecule, annealing, crystallization*.

2. Distinguish between the physical and the chemical properties of matter.

3. Explain *capillary attraction*.
4. Explain the hydrometer.
5. Give the laws of refraction of light.
6. Explain the action of the eye and name its parts.

EXAMINATION X.

1. Define matter; give an example of its three states.
2. Name the universal properties, and define three of them.
3. Name the two kinds of friction, and mention some of the advantages of the same.
4. Define capillarity, and state the law of elevation of liquids in tubes of different sizes.
5. State the law governing the time of oscillation of pendulums of different lengths. Ex. Length 39′ and 156′; required ratio of oscillation.
6. A rifle ball leaves the earth perpendicularly with a velocity of 80 feet per second. Over what distance did it pass?
7. A photometer (define) indicates a sixteen candle-power for a gas-jet 1 foot from a wall. What will be its candle-power 4 feet from the wall?
8. What is the velocity of light? By whom and by what means was it discovered?
9. Explain the construction of the human eye.
10. Explain the construction of a plate electrical machine.

EXAMINATION XI.

1. Describe an experiment illustrating inertia.
2. Define center of gravity. Can the center of gravity be outside of a body?
3. What is meant by specific gravity?
4. How far will a body fall in ten seconds? In half a second?

5. Explain the siphon.
6. Can heat be converted into anything else? How applied in the arts?
7. Telephone.

EXAMINATION XII.

1. Explain the molecular condition in solids, in liquids, in gases, and the transformation from one of these forms to another.
2. Why, when a tumbler is inclined, does the contained water flow down the side instead of falling vertically? Give other example of a similar nature.
3. Why is it that, as usually weighed, a pound of feathers and a pound of lead are not absolutely of the same weight?
4. Illustrate the meaning of the terms: foot pound, kinetic, energy and convection.
5. Explain the paradox that freezing is a heating process and thawing a cooling process.
6. Describe some simple experiments which illustrate the refraction of light.
7. Compare the construction and use of the ordinary thermometer with that of the barometer.
8. Explain the "Angle of Declination" and also some simple manner in which this angle may be shown.
9. Explain the construction and action of a dynamo-electrical machine.
10. Write upon the topics:
   1. The pendulum.
   2. Sound.

EXAMINATION XIII.

1. Define specific gravity. Give method of finding the specific gravity of a solid.
2. Will a vacuum transmit sound? Light? Heat? Why?
3. At what distance above the earth would a man weighing 225 pounds at surface, weigh only 100 pounds?

NATURAL PHILOSOPHY. 217

4. The power-arm of a lever is 10 feet; the weight-arm is 5 feet. (a) How long will the lever be if it is of the first class? (b) Second class? (c) Third class?

5. What is an electro-magnet? Explain its use in the telegraph instrument.

6. Explain the action of the "sun-glass."

7. Give the law of magnetic attraction.

EXAMINATION XIV.

1. Illustrate by diagrams the different levers; assign, values and find results.

2. A stone weighs 12 lbs. in air and 10 lbs. in water; find the specific gravity.

3. Draw simple figure illustrating the hydrostatic press; assign values and find result.

4. Give the name and effect of different kinds of mirrors.

5. Give the name and the effect of the different kinds of lenses.

6. Explain the plilosophy of the ice cream freezer.

7. State the different ways of generating electricity for practical purposes and explain the method commonly used for lights.

EXAMINATION XV.

1. Through which of the three kinds of levers can most power be gained?

2. Through which very little or none? Why? Why do we use this class?

3. A ball projected vetically upwards returns in 15 seconds to the place of projection; how far did it ascend?

4. State the general principle on which hydrostatic pressure depends.

5. State an essential structural difference between the mercurial thermometer and the mercurial barometer.

6. What, if any. is the difference in motion of particles in the transmission of light waves and of sound waves?

7. With figure locate conjugate foci in case of concave mirror.

8. How can specific gravity of bodies lighter than water be ascertained?

9. Name the different kinds of electricity and give an application of each.

EXAMINATION XVI.

1. Define physics and give the philosophy of the three states of matter.

2. What is meant by the specific gravity of a substance? How is the specific gravity of silver found? Of cork?

3. What is temperature? How is it measured? Specific heat.

4. Explain the process of telegraphing. To what uses has electricity lately been put?

5. Transmission of sound.

6. Reflection of light.

EXAMINATION XVII.

1. Define and illustrate two specific properties of matter; two general properties of matter.

2. Name three ways in which heat is transmitted, and give an illustration of each.

3. (1) Describe the pendulum. (2) Two pendulums are respectively 16 and 144 in., what is their proportional time of vibration?

4. State three laws of light.

5. Describe the hydrostatic press.

6. Show by diagram or description the essential parts of the lifting pump.

7. The diameter of a wheel is 7 feet and of the axle 6 inches. What weight, on a cord passing over the wheel

NATURAL PHILOSOPHY. 219

will balance 100 lbs. suspended by a cord passing over the axle?

8. Mention two simple implements involving different mechanical powers, and state which mechanical power each illustrates.

9. On the subject of sound give and explain two laws which govern pitch, or the number of vibrations.

10. Discuss the magnet.

EXAMINATION XVIII.

1. Explain and illustrate the parallelogram of forces.

2. A body that would weigh 194 lbs. at the equator would weigh 195 lbs. at poles. Why?

3. What is specific gravity, and how is specific gravity of liquids found?

4. How is the rainbow produced and why is it circular?

5. How does a lightning rod protect from the effects of lightning?

6. Name the physical properties of matter and discuss malleability.

EXAMINATION XIX.

1. What is Pascal's law in regard to the pressure of liquids.

2. Give the total pressure on the inside of a cubical box 2 feet each way filled with water.

3. Describe briefly the method of finding the specific gravity of a solid that sinks in water.

4. Describe the different forms of water wheels; upon what consideration would the availibility of each depend?

5. Mention five facts in regard to the atmosphere which the air-pump enables us to demonstrate.

6. Describe the action of the hydraulic ram.

7. Describe an incandescent electric light; an arc light.

8 How would you teach the elements of physics to an ignoramus?

EXAMINATION XX.

1. State some of the laws of gravitation.
2. If a body weighs a ton at the surface of the earth, what will it weigh one thousand miles below the surface; and how much one thousand miles above the surface?
3. Give the law of the descent of falling bodies, and what is the velocity of a stone that has been falling ten seconds?
4. What is the distance of lightning when the flash is seen ten seconds before the thunder is heard?
5. Give the three laws of motion?
6. Describe the eye and name its parts.
7. Define specific gravity, and give the law for finding the specific gravity of a solid.
8. What is the specific gravity of gold?
9. What is the undulating theory of light?
10. Draw and describe the telephone?

22. BOTANY.

A Study of the Text-Book and an Analysis of a Certain Number of Specimens.

BOTANY.

EXAMINATION I.

1. Describe the structure of a leaf, and give the office of the foliage in the plant economy. What transformations may the leaves undergo? Illustrate by examples.

2. Describe the growth of the young oak from the acorn, and state clearly what you mean by each of the terms employed. What is a plant?

3. How may you determine whether a plant is endogenous or exogenous? Name three endogens and seven exogens of this vicinity.

4. Give an outline of the parts of a perfect flower, and describe all the parts. How many flowers deviate from the type? Name terms employed in classifying fruits.

5. What is meant by the term aestivation? When is a leaf acuminate? Cordate? When is the corolla called valvate?

6. Name some plants of which we eat the calyx, the fleshy root, the leaves, the stem; the starch of the seed. What parts of plants do men use for clothing?

EXAMINATION II.

1. Define structural botany and angiospermous and gymnospermous plants.

2. Describe the developments of a bean into a young plant with two permanent leaves.

3. Define the kinds of inflorescence and give examples.

4. State the functions of the leaf, the corolla, the stigma and another.

BOTANY. 223

5. Define the classes of fruit as to texture and give an example of each class.

6. What are the essential parts of the plant and what are the functions of each?

7. Comparing the leaf of the maple, the plantain and the mountain ash, what differences do we observe?

8. In what way do the following plants climb: grapes, hops, beans, peas, ivy?

9. Describe the plant given you.

10. Define complete, perfect, symmetrical and regular flower.

11. Describe a tuber, corymb, bulb, and give an example of each.

12. Comparing the cross-section of a corn stalk with that of a maple what peculiarities do we notice? What do they indicate? To what classification do they lead?

EXAMINATION III.

1. State fully the difference between phenogamous and cryptogamous plants in structure and fructifying process.

2. Give different kinds of embryo as regards number of cotyledons. Examples.

3. Classify and sub-classify stems, and illustrate growth.

4. Discuss following parts of a flower: (a) Floral envelope, (b) Essential organs, (c) Torus and receptacle.

5. State functions of leaf of plant.

6. Show how cells are produced.

7. What are the chemical constituents of plants and how are they discovered?

8. What are the characteristics of the Claytonia family?

EXAMINATION IV.

1. Describe leaves as to arrangememrt, outline and form.

2. The food of the plant: What is it, how taken, how assimilated?

3. Describe the fertilization of the ovary and the reproduction of the plant.
4. What is alburnum and when does it become duramen?
5. Describe the growth of the embryo.
6. Give the classification of fruits.

EXAMINATION V.

1. In what respects are a plant and an animal alike? In what respects are they unlike?
2. Give the functions of the root, stem, leaf and flower.
3. What is meant by cohesion in botany? By adhesion?
4. Discuss the subject of fertilization.
5. Name the various parts of a complete flower. State the purpose of each part, and give a full description of them.
6. Define embryo, cotyledon, bud, fruit, androecium and gynoecium.
7. Name the different kinds of subterranean stems and branches and define the different kinds of venation.
8. Name the different kinds of fleshy fruit, and three kinds of dry fruit
9. Explain how plants produce all the food of animals.
10. Name the different kinds of bark, and state what the living parts of a tree are.

EXAMINATION VI.

1. Name and define the two grand divisions of the vegetable kingdom.
2. Define terms endogen, exogen, acrogen, thallogen, and give examples of each.
3. What are the general forms of venation? Give examples.
4. What are the main points of difference between a

plant and an animal: (1) As to their composition, (2) Their structure, (3) Their nutrition?

5. State what part of the plant you eat when you eat potatoes, onions, cabbage, strawberries, celery, watermelons, opium.

EXAMINATION VII.

1. What is botany? Structural botany? Systematic botany?

2. Name, describe and diagram each part of a perfect flower.

3. Distinguish a prickle from a thorn, and give a well-known example of each.

4. Explain terms--tendril, petiole, embryo, corymb, and cryptogamia.

5. From memory, write out the analysis of some flower heretofore considered, belonging to the Rose family.

EXAMINATION VIII.

1. Define plant, and tell the difference between a plant and an animal or a mineral and tell how a plant is affected by cultivation.

2. Define the two grand divisions of the vegetable kingdom—the phaenogamia and the cryptogamia; and tell how they are distinguished.

3. Define root, and tell its office to the plant. Describe the different forms.

4. Define stem, and tell wherein it differs from the root.

5. Define digestion in plants, where and how is it performed?

EXAMINATION IX.

1. Describe the different kinds of woody tissue, and mention the plants and parts of plants, where they are respectively found.

2. Describe the parts seen in the transverse section of a dicotyledonous stem one year old.

3. Define a rhizome, creeping stem, tuber, bulb, corm and tubercle.

4. What is the difference between indeterminate and determinate inflorescence? Enumerate the kinds of each respectively.

5. Describe the structure and development of the anther.

6. Give the essential characters of the following natural orders: malvaceæ, rosaceæ, compositeæ, polygonaceæ, iridaceæ, and melanthaceæ.

EXAMINATION X.

1. Name and define the departments of botany.
2. How are plants distinguished as to their term of life? Give examples.
3. The plant of the flower.
4. Explain the process of germination.
5. The leaf.

EXAMINATION XI.

1. Define botany.
2. Define endogen, exogen, acrogen, thallogen, monocotyledon, and give an example of each.
3. Define di-cotyledon, poly-cotyledon and give an example of each.
4. Name the various parts of a flower, and its essential organs.
5. Define caryopis, drupe, pepo, pome, and legume, and give an example of each.
6. What are the general forms of venation, and which is found on endogenous plants?
7. Name the various forms of leaf margins, and give five forms of leaves.

EXAMINATION XII.

In each of the following couplets select one subject and discuss it carefully:

BOTANY. 227

1. { 1. Leaves.
    2. Flowers.
2. { 1. Stems.
    2. Roots.
3. { 1. Germination.
    2. Growth.
4. { 1. Phænogamia.
    2. Cryptogamia.
5. { 1. Analysis of plants.
    2. Microscopic structure of plants.
6. { 1. Respiration of plants.
    2. Vital processes involved in plant life.
7. { 1. Linnæan system of plant analysis.
    2. Natural system of plant analysis.
8. { 1. The relation of plants to animals.
    2. The relation of botany to other sciences.
9. { 1. The value of botany as a means of mental discipline.
    2. Plant work in primary classes.

EXAMINATION XIII.

1. What is a plant?
2. What is the food of a plant?
3. Define assimilation; under what conditions does it occur?
4. What is the fruit? How many kinds? Examples of each.
5. Explain how the sap is conveyed from the roots to the branches.
6. What changes occur in the ovule to make it a seed?
7. Mention the rings of an exogenous stem. Which are alive?
8. Name the organs of the flower. Tell the use of each.
9. What parts of plants does man use for clothing? For food?
10. How many plants have you analyzed?

EXAMINATION XIV.

1. Distinguish between structural botany and morphology.
2. What is the difference between an endogenous and an exogenous stem?
3. Discuss the embryogenesis of the pistil.
4. Discuss ovule and the embryo in the ovule.
5. Define protoplosm, proliferous, procumbent, polyphyllous, polygynous.

EXAMINATION XV.

1. The structure and growth of the rudimentary plantlet.
2. What knowledge may you gain of the parent plant by inspecting a grain of corn.
3. The plant of a typical flower.
4. Inflorescence and the law upon which it depends.
5. Is the strawberry a fruit in the strict botanical sense? Explain.
6. Enumerate the successive steps which you follow in the analysis of a plant.
7. Give a few characteristics of:
    1. Anemone Thalictroides.
    2. Claytonia Virginica.
    3. Erythronium Americanum.

EXAMINATION XVI.

1 Define shrub, tuber, corn, cell, absorption, assimilation.
2. Name the stages of growth in the life of a plant.
3. Define venation and tell its general forms.
4. Which is found in the endogenous plant?
5. Name the parts of a flower and give the essential organs.
6. How does a complete flower differ from a symmetrical flower?

7. Name and draw three different shapes of leaves.
8. Define the different classes of fruits.
9. Give the leading characteristics of two distinct families and name a plant in each.
10. Name two plants that you have analyzed and give their peculiarities.

EXAMINATION XVII.

1. The general characteristics of the palm tree, how does it differ from our trees?
2. When is a plant a perennial? How does it differ from an annual. Which are typical perennials?
3. State the various functions of the leaf.
4. Explain what is meant by a typical flower. Point out a few exceptions among plants.
5. Define the terms stomates, truncate, pericarp, runcinate and apetalous.
6. Describe in full some plant that is a native of this locality.

EXAMINATION XVIII.

1. Name and define the two grand divisions of plants and give the number of classes included in each.
2. State the function of the leaf, the corolla, the stigma, and the anther.
3. Mention two ways in which propogation takes place in flowering plants.
4. What is assimilation? In what organs does assimilation in plants mainly take place?
5. Give the organs of nutrition and the organs of reproduction of plants.
6. Describe five endogens among our cultivated plants.
7. Tell to what families the following belong, lavender, celery, clover, cotton, apple.
8. Compare the horse chestnut, and the apple in regard to leaf, flower and fruit.

EXAMINATION XIX.

1. Describe the essential organs of a flower.
2. The stages of plant life.
3. Absorption and circulation.
4. How many plants have you analyzed? Describe one of these plants.
5. Name two plants of different families, and tell how they differ.

EXAMINATION XX.

1. Describe the essential organs of a flower.
2. The stages of plant life.
3. Absorption and circulation.
4. How many plants have you analyzed?? Describe one of these plants.
5. Name two plants of different families, and tell who they differ.

EXAMINATION XXI.

1. How does a plant grow?
2. What is a flower? State the uses of the different parts of a flower.
3. Plant food and assimilation.
4. Describe a plant that you have analyzed.
5. Name two plants of different families, and tell how they differ.

EXAMINATION XXII.

1. Name the floral organs and describe one of them.
2. What is the difference between a stem and a root?
3. Describe the various modes of leaf arrangement.
4. Describe a pinnate leaf; a palmate leaf.
5. Describe the parts of an exogenous stem.

EXAMINATION XXIII.

1. Define botany.
2. How would you teach the subject to a child?

3. What relation exists between the seed leaves (cotyledons) and the after leaves of a plant?

4. Why is the rotation : corn, oats, wheat, unscientific?

5. Classify any species of the Ranunculaceae family from memory.

EXAMINATION XXIV.

1. Define herb, shrub, tree, endogenous and exogenous plants.

2. Describe germination, assimilation.

EXAMINATION XXV.

1. Name the distinguishing characteristics of the stem of plants.

2. What are the only living parts of a tree?

3. Give the difference between exogen and endogen.

4. Give the structure of the stem of the apple tree.

5. Explain what is meant by venation.

6. What do the terms regular, symmetrical, perfect and complete mean, as applied to flowers?

7. Define legume, berry, drupe, caryopsis, didynamous.

8. Name and describe a family of plants.

9. Of what does the scientific name of a plant consist? Give an example.

10. Name and define some terms applied to the margin of leaves.

11. Name the parts of the corolla, calyx, stamen, pistil.

EXAMINATION XXVI.

1. Define botany.

2. What is meant by the flora of a country?

3. Name and describe the leaves and essential organs of a flower, and name at least one flower that you have analyzed.

4. Name the parts of the pistil and state what each part performs.

5. Name the parts of a leaf; describe parallel-veined and netted veined leaves.

6. What is assimilation? In what part of the plant and when does it go on? What is the principal gas consumed by plants?

EXAMINATION XXVII.

1. What two kinds of beings compose the organic world, and what are the differences and similarities existing between them?

2. What is the difference in the growth of roots and stems?

3. What are the organs of growth in a plant and what use does each sub-serve?

4. What are the parts of a leaf and of what two kinds of material does it consist?

5. How are leaves named according to their outline?

6. What is a raceme? Corymb? Umbel?

7. Describe a perfect flower and give the uses of each part concerned in fertilization?

8. What is the difference between an imperfect and an incomplete flower?

9. Name the different kinds of fruits and give examples of each?

10. Define the terms endogenous, and exogenous and how can the age of an exogenous tree be determined?

23. GEOMETRY.

Plane Only---First Two Books in Junior Year and Completed in Senior Year.

GEOMETRY.

EXAMINATION I.

1. Let $\begin{smallmatrix}1&3\\|&|\\|&|\\|&|\\2&4\end{smallmatrix}$ be parallel lines. Show that a line cutting them will make equal alternate interior angles.

2. Illusrtate (a) segment; (b) secant; (c) locus; (d) complementary angles.

3. The diagonals of an isosceles trapezoid are equal.

4. The sum of the interior angles of a polygon is equal to what? Prove.

5. Define and illustrate (a) locus; (b) incommensurable quantities; (c) median; (d) similar figures.

6. Construct a parallelogram equivalent to a given trapezoid.

7. Given a map of the western hemisphere, draw a true meridian passing through New York.

8. Triangles having their sides respectively proportional are similar.

9. The perpendiculars from the vertices of a triangle to the opposite sides meet in a point. Let the triangle be

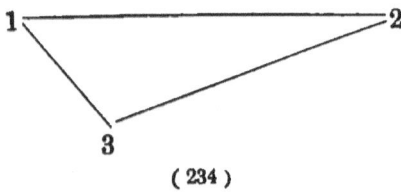

GEOMETRY. 235

EXAMINATION II.

1. Show that the square described on the hypothenuse of a right-angled triangle is equal to the sum of the squares on the other two sides.
2. Define similar triangles and prove that they are to each other as the squares of their homologous sides.
3. Prove that the diagonals of a parallelogram bisect each other.
4. How much larger is a square circumscribing a circle 40 rods in diameter than a square inscribed in the same circle?
5. Suppose the length of this room is 36 feet, width 33 feet, height 14 feet. What is the distance from the N. E. upper corner to the S. W. lower corner.
6. A ring is made in a field 100 feet square. Find the area of the land left in the corners.

EXAMINATION III.

1. Draw and define all the different forms of the quadrilateral.
2. Prove that in every triangle the sum of the three angles is equal to two right angles.
3. If $a : b : : c : d$, prove that $am : bn : : cm : dn$.
4. Prove that the square described on the hypothenuse of a right-angled triangle is equal to the sum of the squares of the other two sides.
5. Show how at a given point in a straight line to erect a perpendicular to that line.
6. Prove that the area of a circle is equal to the circumference multiplied by one-half the radius.
7. Prove that a perpendicular is the shortest line which can be drawn from a point to a plane.
8. A man has a square yard containing $\frac{1}{10}$ of an acre; he makes a gravel walk around it which occupies $\frac{1}{64}$ of the whole yard; what is the width of the walk?

EXAMINATION IV.

1. The sum of the three angles of a triangle equals two right angles.
2. A straight railway passes two miles from a town. A place is four miles from town and one mile from the railway. Find by construction how many places answer this description. Construct figure.
3. If $5x=9y$, what is the ratio of x to y?
4. If $a:b::c:d$ prove that $a+b:a-b::c+d:c-d$.
5. If from a point without a circle a tangent and a secant be drawn, the tangent is a mean proportional between the whole secant and the part without the circle.
6. Find the area of a circle whose sides are 73, 57, and 48 inches respectively.
7. In a park there is a circular drive whose outer circumference is 654 yds. 2 ft. 7.2 inches, while its inner circumference is 610 yds. 2 ft. 7.2 inches. How wide is the drive?

EXAMINATION V.

1. Prove that the exterior angle of a triangle is equal to the two interior opposite angles.
2. Prove that if one acute angle of a rt. triangle is double the other, the hypotenuse is double the shorter leg.
3. Prove that the tangents to a circle from an exterior point are equal, and make equal angles with a line joining the point to the center of the circle.
4. Prove that if an equilateral triangle is inscribed in a circle, the distance from each side to the center of the circle is one-half the radius of the circle.
5. Prove that if four quantities are proportional, they are proportional (1) by inversion; (2) by composition; (3) by division and composition.
6. Prove that the square on the hypothenuse of a rt.

GEOMETRY. 237

triangle is equal to the sum of the squares of the two legs.

7. Prove that the area of a regular polygon is equal to one-half the product of its equal apothem by the perimeter.

8. The dimensions of a rectangular garden are 32x18 rods. Required the diameter of a circular garden of equal area.

9. A circle is inscribed in a government section of land. Required the amount of land within the section and outside the circle.

10. A square park contains 10 acres. How much longer is a side of the square than the distance from the center to one of the corners.

EXAMINATION VI.

1. Draw and define: Angle, trapezoid isosceles triangle, rhombus, scalene triangle.

2. What are all the names applicable to a plane figure whose sides are equal and whose angles are right angles?

3. Prove that circumferences of circles are as their radii, and that their areas as the squares of their radii.

4. Prove that in a r. a. triangle the hypotenuse^2 equals base^2 plus altitude.^{2}

5. When a circle is inscribed in a square it is found that the area of one of the corner spaces between the circumference and sides of the square is 21.46 sq. feet, find the area of the square and of the circle.

6. When a ladder reaches the top of a house its foot is 12 feet from the base of the wall; when the ladder is drawn down four feet from the top of the house its foot is 20 feet from the base of the wall, find length of ladder and height of house without the use of algebra. Draw the figure.

7. A frustum is 20 feet high with bases 30 feet square and 15 feet square. Find its volume and entire surface.

8. The diagonal of a cube is 100 feet. Find volume and surface.

9. The circumference × half the radius equals area of a circle. Demonstrate.

EXAMINATION VII.

1. Define (a) geometry, (b) similar figures, (c) equivalent figures, (d) equal figures, (e) a regular polygon, (f) rhomboid.

2. Prove that two straight lines perpendicular to the same straight line are parallel.

3. Prove: If from a point without a circle a tangent and secant be drawn, the tangent will be a mean proportional between the whole secant and its external segment.

4. State and prove how to find the area of a triangle.

5. Prove the rule for finding the area of a circle.

6. Show how to construct a rectangle whose area is 64 square inches and whose perimeter is 40 inches.

7. How many degrees in each angle of a regular octagon?

8. Divide a line 48 inches long in extreme and mean ratio.

9. Find the volume of a regular pyramid whose altitude is 10 feet and whose base is an equilateral triangle whose sides are 10 inches each.

10. R—————R.
Town A is 5 miles from the railroad R. R. Draw figure and show where those points are situated which are 2 miles from the railroad and 10 miles from the town.

EXAMINATION VIII.

1. Prove the area of the trapezoid.

2. Prove the sum of three angles of any triangle equals —what?

3. Prove the value of each interior angle of a regular decagon.

4. Prove the value of Pi.
5. If $a : b :: c : d$, prove that $(a+b) : (a-b) :: (c+d) : (c-d)$.
6. Show how to find the center of any circle.
7. Prove that the diagonals of a rhombus bisect each other at right angles.
8. How do you bisect a given angle?
9. Prove the square described on the hypothenuse equals—what?
10. Define similar triangles, rhomboid; and prove the area of a circle equal to the value of Pi into the square of the radius.

EXAMINATION IX.

1. Prove that any two sides of a triangle are together greater than the third.
2. Are the triangles whose sides are proportioned to 2, 3, 4, and 3, 4, 5, respectively right-angled or not?
3. Prove that the area of a rhombus is equal to half the rectangle contained by the diagonals.
4. When is a straight line said to touch a circle? What is a segment of a circle.
5. If $a : b :: c : d$, prove that $am : bn :: cm : dn$.
6. What is the difference in area between a rectangle 60 ft. by 40 ft., and a square which has the same perimeter?
7. What are the three regular figures which can be used in paving a plane area? Show that no regular figures but these will fill up a space round a point.

EXAMINATION X.

1. Define a plane, a right angle, a perpendicular, vertical angles.
2. Define a postulate, a corollary, a scholium, a demonstration.

3. Define a trapezoid, a quadrilateral, a rhombus, a rectangle.

4. Prove that two right-angled triangles are equal when the hypothenuse and an acute angle of the one are equal to a hypothenuse and an acute angle of the other.

5. Write the propositions relating to the measurement of angles.

6. If from any point in the base of an isosceles triangle, parallels to the equal sides be drawn, show that a parallelogram is formed whose perimeter is equal to the equal sides of the triangle.

7. Show that the side of a circumscribed equilateral triangle is double the side of an inscribed equilateral triangle.

8. BAC is a triangle having the angle B double the angle A. If BD bisect the angle and meet AC in D, show that BD is equal to AD.

9. If $A:B::C:D$, and $B:D::m:n$, prove that $A-m:A+m::C-n:C+n$.

EXAMINATION XI.

1. Prove that the diagonals of a parallelogram bisect each other.

2. An inscribed angle is measured by one-half of the arc intercepted by its sides.

3. The three bisectors of the three angles of a triangle meet in a point.

4. To inscribe in a given circle a regular hexagon.

5. To describe a circumference through three points not in the same straight line.

6. Prove the value of the interior angle of a regular octagon.

7. Given the distance between the diagonal and the side of a square, to construct the square.

GEOMETRY. 241

8. The perpendicular distance between two parallels is 30 and a line is drawn across them at an angle of 45 degrees. What is the length between the parallels.

EXAMINATION XII.

1. Enunciate three theorems pertaining to the measurement of surfaces.
2. Prove the theorem in geometry that you like best.
3. If a : b :: c : d :: e : f, show that a : b :: a+c+e : b+d+f.
4. Draw a circumference through three points not in the same straight line.

EXAMINATION XIII.

1. The sum of the three angles of a triangle is equal to two right angles.
2. If four quantities are in proportion, they are in proportion by division.
3. An inscribed angle is measured by half the intercepted arc.
4. Similar triangles are to each other as the squares of their homologous sides.
5. The square described on the hypothenuse of a right-angled triangle is equivalent to the sum of the squares on the other two sides.
6. Problem—To inscribe a circle in a given triangle.
7. Find the value of each interior angle ot a regular decagon.
8. Prove that if the three sides of an equilateral triangle are produced, all the external acute angles are equal and all the obtuse angles are equal.

EXAMINATION XIV.

1. If the line bisecting the vertical angle of a triangle also bisect the base, show that the triangle is isosceles?

2. How many degrees in each angle of a regular hexagon?

3. State three propositions relating to the measurement of angles and prove one of them.

4. To construct a mean proportional to two given lines.

EXAMINATION XV.

1. Two triangles are equal when three sides of one are respectively equal to three sides of the other.

2. A straight line cannot intersect the circumference of a circle in more than two points.

3. Two triangles which have their sides respectively perpendicular to each other are similar.

4. Similar triangles are to each other as the squares of their homologous sides.

5. Inscribe a circle in a given triangle.

EXAMINATION XVI.

1. Define plane, angle, postulate, sector, similar polygons. Name, describe and illustrate the different quadrilaterals.

2. If two sides of a quadrilateral are equal and parallel, the figure is a parallelogram. Demonstrate.

3. A straight line perpendicular to a radius at its extremity is tangent to the circle at that point. State and prove converse also.

4. The square described on the hypothenuse of a right triangle is equivalent to the sum of the squares described on the other two sides. First proof.

EXAMINATION XVII.

1. Define a plane surface. An angle. A polygon. A theorem. The focus of a point. If an angle is three-fifths of a right angle, how many degrees in its supplement? In its complement?

GEOMETRY. 243

2. If two angles of a triangle are equal, what can you say of the sides opposite the equal angles? Of the triangle. Give proof.

3. What is the sum of the interior angles of a polygon? Give proof.

4. Prove that in the same circle, or in equal circles, equal chords are equally distant from the center, and of two unequal chords, the less is farther from the center

5. Draw a right triangle. Draw a perpendicular from the vertex of the right angle to the hypotenuse.
   a. Prove that the triangles thus formed are similar.
   b. Between what two lines is the perpendicular a mean proportional? Give proof.
   c. Between what two lines is the shorter side a mean proportional? Give proof.
   d. What two lines have the same ratio as the squares on the sides of the right triangle? Give proof.

6. Prove that the area of a trapezoid is equal to one-half the sum of the parallel sides multiplied by the altitude. Can you show that your demonstration rests upon geometrical concepts and axioms?

7. Prove that the area of a circle is equal to one-half the product of its radius by its circumference. Upon what does this demonstration depend?

8. How can the area of an irregular polygon be found? Illustrate by drawing figure.

9. Divide a triangle into three equal parts by lines drawn from a point in one of its sides.

10. Of what use to the public school teacher is the study of Geometry?

EXAMINATION XVIII.

1. Prove the sum of three angles of any triangle equals —what?

2. If $a : b : : c : d$, prove that $a + b : a - b : : c + d : c - d$.

3. Prove the area of the trapezoid.
4. Show how to find the center of any circle.
5. Prove the value of *Pi*. Or area of the circle.
6. Prove that the square described on the hypothenuse equals—what?
7. A man has a circular garden and his wife has a square one, and each garden contains one acre, how much further around is one than the other?
8. The gable ends of a house are each 48 feet wide, and the perpendicular height of the ridge above the eaves is 10 feet; how many feet of boards will it take to board up both gables?

EXAMINATION XIX.

1. Define the following terms: chord, tangent, sector, segment, similar figures, equal figures, equivalent figures.
2. In the equilateral triangle ABC, prove the external angle formed by AC, and BC produced, is bisected by CE drawn parallel to the third side AB.
3. Prove that in a right-angled triangle, the line drawn from the vertex of the right angle to the middle of the hypotenuse is equal to one-half of the hypotenuse.
4. DEF is a triangle having the angle E twice as great as the angle F; if E G bisect the angle E and meet DF in G, prove that EG is equal to GF.
5. AB, a chord of a circle, is the base of an isosceles triangle whose vertex, C, is outside the circle and whose equal sides cut the circumferece in D and E. Prove that CE is equal to CD.
6. An angle measured by the intersection of two chords is measured by what? Demonstrate.
7. If from BD, the diagonal of the square ABCD, BE be cut off equal to BC, and EF be drawn perpendicular to BD at E, prove that DE will be equal to EF and also equal to FC.

GEOMETRY. 245

8. If the four sides of a quadrilateral be bisected, the lines joining the points of bisection will form a parallelogram. Prove it of a trapezium.

EXAMINATION XX.

1. Define geometry, demonstration, theorem, problem, axiom. Give axioms.
2. If two parallel straight lines be cut by a third straight line, the alternate interior angles are equal, the exterior interior angles are equal, the sum of the two interior angles on the same side of the secant line is equal to two right angles.
3. To inscribe a circle in a given triangle.
4. If two polygons are similar, they are composed of the same number of triangles which are similar and are similarly placed.
5. The area of a circle is equal to one-half the product of the radius by its circumference.—Cor. 1.
6. The square described on the hypothenuse of a right-angled triangle is equal to the sum of the squares on the other two sides.
7. In the same circle or in equal circles, incommensurable arcs have the same ratio as the angles which they subtend at the center.

EXAMINATION XXI.

1. Outline plane figures.
2. Define angle, surface, plane, parallel lines, adjacent angles, alternate angles, reentrant angle. Illustrate.
3. If a line has two points each equally distant from the extremities of a line, it is perpendicular. Prove.
4. Through 3 points not in a straight line, what may be made to pass. Prove.
5. Show how to measure an angle having its vertex in the circumference of a circle.

6. Prove that the sum of all the angles of any triangle is 180°.

7. Given $a : b :: c : d$. Prove $a : na + mb :: c : nc + md$.

EXAMINATION XXII.

1. Define plane, polygon, square, rhomboid, rhombus, similar polygons.

2. The sum of the exterior angles of a polygon—

3. The measure of an angle having vertex at the circumference of a circle—

4. The area of a circle—what?

5. Prove that area of a circle—

6. The square on the side of a triangle opposite the acute angle—

7. What is the number of degrees in the angles of a regular octagon?

10. A man has a square garden and his wife a circular one, each containing one acre, how many yds. further is one around than the other?

EXAMINATION XXIII.

1. Define geometry, line, point altitude, theorem, chord.

2. The area of a triangle is half the product of its base and altitude. Demonstrate.

3. The sum of the angles of a triangle is two right angles. Demonstrate.

4. What is the sum of the angles of a nonagon? What is the value of one of the angles of a regular nonagon? Of an exterior angle.

5. The area of a regular polygon is equal to one-half of its apothem into its perimeter. Demonstrate.

6. In a circle whose radius is 20, what is the length of an arc of a sector whose angle is 30°? What is the area of the sector?

7. Find the side of a square inscribed in a circle whose diameter is 5 feet.

GEOMETRY. 247

EXAMINATION XXIV.

1. Define axiom, corollary, scholium, plane, quadrilateral, alternation and inversion (Illustrate with proportion), chord, sector, segment (Illustrate 7, 8 and 9 with figures), similar polygons.

2. Draw and name all the quadrilaterals.

3. If the diagonals of a quadrilateral bisect each other, at right angles, prove that the figure is a rhombus or a square.

4. Prove that the perimeters of similar polygons are to each other as any two homologous sides and the polygons to each other as the squares of those sides.

5. Prove that if a straight line is perpendicular to a radius at its (outer) extremity, it will be tangent to the circle at that point, and conversely.

ANNOUNCEMENT.

It was not deemed best to publish answers to the questions in this book. They would destroy its value as a means of original investigation, which the compilers consider its chief value. THE SCHOOL GAZETTE will cheerfully answer any questions about which the reader may be in doubt.

www.ingramcontent.com/pod-product-compliance
Lightning Source LLC
Chambersburg PA
CBHW020803230426
43666CB00007B/830